BUILDING MENTAL TOUGHNESS

7 Practical Steps to Develop the Best Mindset for Peak
Performance—Improve Self-Discipline, Boost
Confidence, Stop Overthinking

AMBER PRESTON

Table of Contents

Introduction

Life has a way of throwing curveballs when we least expect it. One moment, everything seems to be going smoothly—you're coasting along, handling your responsibilities, enjoying time with friends and family. The next moment, bam! A sudden challenge blindsides you, whether it's a strained relationship, a financial setback, or a personal loss. In times like these, you desperately yearn for an inner resilience that could help you bounce back. Instead, you feel emotionally brittle, like a thin sheet of ice that might crack at the slightest provocation.

This feeling of fragility often leaves you spinning in an endless loop of anxiety and self-doubt. You berate yourself for not being "tough enough"—strong enough to handle adversity with some semblance of grace. If only you could develop a thicker emotional hide, you tell yourself, you wouldn't crumble at every obstacle. So you try to suppress your difficult emotions through work, social media, or yet another Netflix binge. But the discontent lingers—a splinter in your mind.

If this experience resonates with you, you're not alone. We all want to believe we can muscle through challenges with stoic grit like some movie superhero. But real mental strength isn't about acting tough; it's about building emotional resilience through self-awareness and adaptability. Without understanding the root of our feelings and developing healthy coping mechanisms, any façade of toughness will eventually crack.

This book holds the keys to cultivating authentic, long-lasting mental strength accessible to anyone willing to do the soul-searching work. In *Building Mental Toughness*, I provide a 7-step training program for building mental muscle—not just surviving life's curveballs but thriving because of them. Through relatable storytelling and gentle guidance, you uncover how to

- rewire habitual thought patterns causing anxiety and overthinking
- develop confidence through vulnerability and self-compassion
- establish emotional boundaries for improved self-worth
- cultivate optimism and positivity whatever life brings

And so much more! Unlike restrictive one-size-fits-all solutions, the book offers tailored techniques for people across backgrounds and temperaments. You discover a versatility that enables you not just to power through challenges but grow because of them.

So, what's the catalyst for picking up this book? Well, ask yourself:

Do I tend to crumble when faced with obstacles, great and small?

Does adversity often plunge me into a pit of panic and gloom?

Would I like to handle life's curveballs with more emotional agility?

If you answered yes, then this book likely landed in your hands for a reason. Perhaps you're tired of living at the mercy of external ups and downs. Or maybe you want mental resilience not just for yourself but to model for your children. Whatever the catalyst, know that investing in this journey will provide dividends for years to come.

By reading this book, you're not just developing grit; you're reinventing life on your own terms. You discover lasting techniques to handle uncertainty, heal from hardship, and boldly pursue your aspirations. Instead of hiding your sensitivity, you leverage it for personal transformation.

Imagine showing up for your challenges with unflinching courage and optimism. Envision bouncing back from failures with renewed passion. Consider how self-trust and confidence could ripple through all areas of your life.

This all begins with the first step detailed in "Chapter 2: Stop Overthinking in its Tracks." Along the way, I will guide you with compassionate firmness—as the coach who believes in you more than you believe in yourself. Each carefully designed chapter concludes with inspiring real-world stories, reinforcing that change is truly possible.

If empowering yourself with unassailable mental strength sounds appealing, then join me on this life-changing journey of self-discovery and growth. This book builds upon the concepts introduced in *Mastering Emotional Intelligence With Ease*, providing additional insights and strategies to help you navigate life's challenges. However, even if you haven't read the previous book, you'll find valuable information and guidance within these pages. With the roadmap you'll soon find, adversity only makes you sharper, distress deepens your wisdom, and the obstacles once weighing you down have become catalysts for positive transformation. The life you've always imagined is closer than you think.

ONE

Understanding Mental Toughness

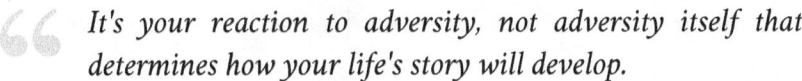 *It's your reaction to adversity, not adversity itself that determines how your life's story will develop.*

Dieter F. Uchtdorf

Life has a peculiar way of testing our mettle when we least expect it. Without warning, an unexpected challenge drops into our lap, and suddenly, we find ourselves face-to-face with adversity. Perhaps you've lost a job, ended a relationship, dealt with grief, or faced discrimination. In these turbulent times, you desperately wish you had nerves of steel and unshakable composure. But instead, you discover you're emotionally fragile—stressed, doubtful, and overwhelmed.

If this experience resonates with you, take comfort in knowing you're not alone. We all hope we'd face our firewalk unflinchingly, but the truth is, adversity often catches us off-guard, revealing our emotional brittleness. What if I told you there was another way?

Beyond just surviving life's curveballs, what if you could thrive because of them, transforming trials into catalysts for growth?

That's exactly what this chapter will help you uncover—the art of mental toughness. And I'm not talking about suppressing emotions or pretending to be invincible. No, this is about building real resilience on multiple levels—your mindset, behavior, and emotional landscape. With this skill, you don't just withstand turbulence; you harness it to elevate your life's trajectory.

Over the course of this chapter, you'll come to intimately understand what mental toughness is, why it matters, and how to cultivate this extraordinary aptitude accessible to us all. Consider this your invitation to stop avoiding adversity and start befriending it on your own terms. Life's obstacles need not break you; they can propel your evolution if you let them. That's the secret this chapter whispers.

We begin our journey by clearly defining mental toughness—what it is and what it is not. With insightful examples and vital background context, you quickly grasp this nebulous concept and all its subtleties. Then, we explore the invaluable role resilience plays in anchoring one's mental strength, especially during storms. You uncover why resilience and toughness are two threads of the same cloth.

As we delve deeper, you gain clarity on common barricades that inhibit mental toughness—from stress and peer pressure to emotional repression. By understanding these obstacles, you're empowered to circumvent them through mindset shifts and coping outlets illuminated later on. Knowledge of barriers is just as crucial as mapping the destination.

This chapter also addresses a pivotal question: What is the linkage between mental health disorders like anxiety, depression, OCD,

Rumination essentially entraps people in a vicious thought cycle that exacerbates and prolongs psychological pain rather than leading to constructive solutions. In the long term, this erosion of emotional equilibrium hampers mental toughness significantly.

Additionally, unchecked stress often goes hand-in-hand with rumination, especially related to work, finances, relationships, trauma, or health issues. While occasional bouts of stress are unavoidable, chronic high stress magnifies emotional turbulence.

Without positive coping outlets, people rely even more heavily on rumination to manage elevated stress and negative emotions. This forms an unhealthy reinforcing loop where stress encourages rumination and rumination intensifies stress. Over time, individuals burn through their resilience reserves faster during crises, making constructive responses challenging.

Rumination and excessive stress are two linked pitfalls that can profoundly deplete our mental toughness, emotional flexibility, and psychological stamina over time if left unmanaged. Learning to reroute rumination while proactively addressing stress is pivotal for resilience.

People Pleasing and Peer Pressure

Many of us have a natural tendency to want approval from others. However, taken to an extreme, people-pleasing tendencies can undermine resilience and mental toughness. When our sense of self-worth rests predominantly on external validation, we become emotionally fragile.

People-pleasers often overextend themselves, trying to meet everyone's expectations. This leads to suppressed inner needs, poor boundaries, and diminished self-care. Unable to say no, they take on increasing burdens until daily life feels chronically overwhelming. This erosion of personal power leaves minimal inner reserves to tackle bigger adversities.

Additionally, the failure to stand firm often draws increasing disrespect from others over time. People-pleasers' inability to voice their true needs trains manipulators how little it takes to coerce them into uncomfortable situations. This further aggravates stress, anxiety, resentment, and despair.

Peer pressure produces similar outcomes. When people-pleasers constantly conform to their peers' desires rather than honoring their own, it breeds inauthenticity and self-betrayal. Not only do they attract peers who pressure them into riskier behaviors, but they also lose touch with their inner compass. This makes it exponentially harder to demonstrate resilience during crises.

In short, people-pleasing and peer pressure tend to lock us into an endless tailspin of external validation-seeking and inner insecurity. This quicksand must be avoided at all costs to develop lasting mental toughness. We must learn to stand confidently in ourselves and walk our own path, no matter how lonely it may be at times. With inner surety comes outer resilience.

Being Cold vs. Being Tough

In striving to become more mentally tough, it's easy to confuse this with being emotionally cold, detached, or unfeeling. However, the two could not be more different. Genuine mental toughness does not require ignoring your emotions; in fact, it relies on embracing the full spectrum of emotions with agility.

Being cold typically involves shutting out or numbing difficult feelings like grief, heartbreak, fear, or vulnerability. People who resort to emotional coldness often do so due to past traumas or attachment issues that left them wary of revealing sensitivity. By keeping others at bay and sealing off their inner world, they shield themselves from recurring hurts.

However, this emotional barricading exacts steep costs: isolation, loneliness, and inability to form intimate bonds. It also tends to fail during life's hardest blows, when suppressed emotions inevitably erupt like pressure cookers. In short, emotional coldness provides the illusion of strength while masking extreme brittleness.

In contrast, mentally tough individuals understand emotions and provide data worth examining, not weaknesses needing eradication. Instead of repressing vulnerability, the emotionally agile leverages it to build deeper connections, gain wisdom, and ask for needed support during rough patches. Rather than disconnecting from their feelings, the mentally tough nurture their entire inner ecosystem for optimum functioning during storms.

While being cold may mistakenly seem like a quick fix for those afraid of emotional overwhelm, it inhibits authentic relationships and lasting resilience. Conversely, mental toughness acknowledges strength and vulnerability are two sides of the same beautiful coin —both essential for living fully and compassionately no matter what comes.

Mental Health

Our mental health status exerts an enormous influence on our capacity for resilience and mental fortitude. When disorders like chronic anxiety, clinical depression, or post-traumatic stress intrude, they chip away at the bedrock supporting the emotional endurance needed to withstand crises.

Anxiety

Anxiety disorders foster prolonged emotional distress, irrational fears, excessive rumination, and avoidant behaviors—all impediments to strength during turbulence. Additionally, research indicates chronic anxiety correlates to reduced resilience after traumatic events due to diminished self-efficacy and learned helplessness (Charney, 2003).

Those suffering from anxiety often struggle to utilize positive reappraisals when faced with situations triggering unease and panic. This inhibits access to inner reserves that facilitate coping. Essentially, anxiety narrows our ability to process challenges logically and demonstrate mental agility.

Depression

Depression's gloomy influence on thought patterns and energy levels can profoundly diminish mental toughness. Those enduring major depressive episodes frequently find past resilience strategies ineffective, as the disorder often severs links between past wins and current self-efficacy.

Additionally, depression is characterized by amplified self-criticism, hopelessness about the future, and isolation from social support—all immunity dampeners when trials strike. By impairing executive function and cognitive flexibility, depression makes summoning our grit exponentially harder.

Other Conditions

Research shows a myriad of other diagnoses, like obsessive-compulsive disorder (OCD), schizophrenia, and borderline personality disorder, often coincide with depleted resilience markers in the wake of adversity (Porter et al., 2019). Additionally, compounding life stressors like divorce, the deaths of loved ones, or economic instability frequently correspond to accelerated erosion of individuals' mental and emotional stamina.

While mental toughness can certainly coexist with mental health issues given appropriate treatment, poor psychological health undoubtedly weakens individuals' baseline ability to withstand and recover from crises. Seeking help through counseling, medication, mindfulness practices, exercise, social connection, and healthy outlets can reinforce reserves.

Wrapping Up...

In this chapter, we've laid the groundwork for deeply comprehending mental toughness—what it entails, why it matters, and how to cultivate it. We've seen that genuine mental strength relies not on emotional repression but on resilience, adaptability, and wisdom in the face of challenges.

We've covered key concepts including

- the principles of mental toughness and its role in resilience
- common obstacles like stress, rumination, and peer pressure
- the impact of mental health on fortifying inner grit
- transforming life's curveballs from crises into catalysts

Understanding mental toughness is setting the foundation for living life undaunted by external turbulence. By recognizing adversity as a school rather than a threat, we open ourselves to profound learning and self-actualization. Equipped with this knowledge, we're now ready to embark upon the seven-step training program for developing unassailable mental strength.

In the next chapter, we begin this journey by tackling the epidemic of overthinking and freeing ourselves from its confines. You'll discover targeted techniques from mindfulness to mental pattern rewiring to gain supremacy over your inner world. Understanding mental toughness provides the vision; cultivating it is where the real work begins.

Case Study: Kate

When Kate lost her high-paying job of over a decade, her world turned upside down. As a single mom, she had depended on that job to provide a comfortable life for her two kids. Now, with her main source of income gone and few prospects on the horizon, she felt utterly overwhelmed and powerless.

Bills were piling up, her kids were stressed, and Kate's own mental health was deteriorating rapidly. She second-guessed all her career choices, wondering if she should have played it safer. Constant anxiety and sleepless nights left her exhausted and despairing. She began to isolate herself, withdrawing from friends and family out of shame.

In this storm of adversity, Kate desperately wished she could be mentally tougher—more resilient, more composed, more hopeful. But the sheer weight of her situation felt like a tidal wave knocking the wind out of her over and over again. She doubted she had the grit to come out of this catastrophe in one piece.

That's when Kate came across a book that talked about genuine mental strength coming not from faking positivity but from acknowledging difficult emotions. It didn't advise her to pretend she wasn't anxious or in financial trouble; it asked her to embrace the full gamut of emotions that accompany hardship. The book spoke to Kate's intuition that mental toughness wasn't about repressing fears or being invincible; it was about building resilience by moving through pain compassionately yet decisively.

Armed with this new perspective, Kate allowed herself to feel the ache of loss when staring at her empty bank account. But she also reminded herself that this intense anxiety would pass and better days awaited. She let tears flow after receiving yet another foreclosure warning but quickly refocused on compiling her resume. She felt the familiar pang of seeing ex-colleagues on social media but consciously shifted her attention to networking events.

The book also cautioned Kate about barriers that could erode mental toughness. Recognizing unhealthy rumination as an obstacle, she turned down the volume on relentless worrying by practicing mindfulness exercises. Scheduling regular meet-ups with supportive friends reinforced her coping mechanisms. Journaling helped her vent emotions and then strategize goals. Kate even tackled an anxiety disorder diagnosis proactively, unwilling to let it undermine her resilience.

Within a few months, Kate was interviewing for new positions with renewed confidence. By allowing herself to fully experience hardship without being debilitated, she emerged wiser and tougher. She landed a job that brought financial stability and even more fulfillment. Kate realized she didn't just want to survive adversity; she wanted to become its master.

Reflecting on her arduous journey, Kate saw everything she gained by walking through the fire—a deeper trust in her own abilities, indispensable coping tools, and profoundly empathetic relationships. She knew that the next life challenge might bring anxiety, but it would no longer bring despair. Kate had found an inner compass that now steered her not around but through troubles with scalpel-sharp awareness and unsinkable poise.

TWO

Step #1—Stop Overthinking in its Tracks

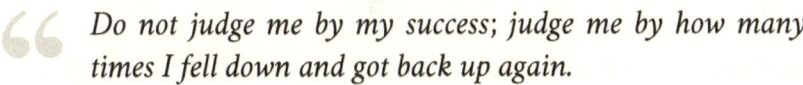

Do not judge me by my success; judge me by how many times I fell down and got back up again.

Nelson Mandela

Nelson Mandela's quote is the perfect mantra as we tackle the common habit of overthinking that keeps tripping us up mentally. In this chapter, we'll explore tools to break this cycle of obsessive worrying so we can get back on our feet stronger than before.

Together, we'll uncover easy yet effective ways to control our runaway thoughts and focus our minds. First, we'll better understand why our brains get hooked on overanalyzing everything and how this drains our mental and emotional energy. You'll learn simple mindfulness practices to catch your thoughts before they spiral and consciously shift your attention to calmer spaces. Additionally, you'll acquire thought-challenging skills to dismantle exaggerated, anxious thinking patterns and rewrite more balanced thought narratives.

As we go, supplementary coping ideas will come to light, including using healthy distractions to disrupt obsessive thoughts. You'll grasp why staying active and productive fights worry. And you'll discover how social bonds can ease anxiety. By the chapter's end, you'll have all the tools to kick overthinking to the curb for good and direct your thoughts toward your true priorities.

So let's start this empowering journey inspired by Mandela's wisdom not to judge ourselves by how often we stumble but by how often we rise back up.

Overthinking 101

If your mind often feels like a broken record, endlessly replaying worries on an anxious loop, you're no stranger to overthinking. But what exactly is this experience we call "overthinking," and how is it sabotaging our mental health? Let's explore its meaning, risks, and origins.

What Is Overthinking?

In short, overthinking refers to excessive, repetitive thoughts focused on negative outcomes, errors, or imperfections. It goes beyond productive problem-solving into unconstructive what-ifs and worst-case scenarios. Our analytical abilities shift from ally to adversary, conjuring exaggerated dangers rather than rational solutions.

Unlike fleeting bouts of everyday worrying, overthinking forms thought spirals that hijack attention for lengthy periods. These mental back-and-forths feed off uncertainty, transitions, perceived threats to ego, and changes beyond one's control—anything that disrupts normalcy. Overthinking entangles people in futile attempts to anticipate, prevent, or mentally resolve non-existent crises. This anguished mental wrestling yields little besides escalating anxiety and despair.

Overthinking vs. Rumination

Overthinking and rumination overlap significantly but have subtle distinctions. Rumination tends to fixate on negative personal traits, past failures, current problems without clear solutions, and bleak future scenarios. It carries a self-judgmental tone of blame and self-criticism.

In contrast, overthinking obsesses primarily over ambiguous external situations with possibly catastrophic implications. The spotlight centers on threat avoidance/mitigation rather than self-reproach. While rumination erodes self-worth, overthinking slowly poisons peace of mind. Both leave mental carnage in their wake.

Dangers of Overthinking

Overthinking unleashes a cascade of destructive consequences that wreak havoc on well-being. Fixating on emotionally charged "what-ifs" triggers chemical changes in the brain, raising stress hormones like cortisol. This heightens bodily sensations of anxiety —racing heart, tense muscles, insomnia. Not only does over-thinking create distress in the moment, but chronic activation of the brain's fear pathways can fundamentally alter its structure and chemistry over time.

Additionally, overthinking often precipitates avoidance of potential emotional triggers or stressful situations. This shrinking social landscape breeds isolation and disconnection. As mood plummets, many fall into clinical anxiety or depression, needing professional treatment. In short, overthinking isn't just mentally exhausting; it's physiologically and emotionally corrosive.

Where Overthinking Comes From

Overthinking does not arise from innate character flaws or weaknesses. In fact, tendencies take root due to three primary causes: childhood conditioning, trauma response, or unsupportive environments. Growing up in chaotic, critical, or emotionally neglectful homes often wires overthinking patterns at a young age. Trauma also commonly triggers hypervigilant thoughts around safety and violation of trust. Additionally, cultural messaging plays a role, along with enabling relationships that reinforce obsessive worry. The seeds of overthinking scatter widely, but self-awareness and care can circumvent their sprouting.

Solution #1: Mindfulness

If your thoughts often feel like a broken record, playing the same worries on a loop, mindfulness can help you press stop. This first powerful solution helps you break free from exhausting mental loops and find inner peace.

What Is Mindfulness?

Mindfulness means focusing your awareness on the present moment. Instead of getting tangled up in regrets about the past or worries about the future, you purposefully redirect your focus to the here and now.

Mindfulness meditation strengthens this ability to stay grounded in the present. As thoughts come and go, you simply acknowledge them without judging them as good or bad. You don't latch onto them or get sucked into mental tunnels. You just gently shift your attention back to the now. This practice builds the mental muscle memory to catch yourself overthinking and hit pause.

How Mindfulness Helps Overthinking

Mindfulness helps in a few key ways. First, it builds awareness of when your mind wanders, preventing you from falling into obsessive thought trains. Noticing unhelpful thoughts early helps stop them from gaining momentum.

Second, mindfulness calms the brain's fear response centers which leads to stressful rumination. This reduces anxiety and boosts clear thinking.

Third, mindfulness reveals thoughts as passing events rather than absolute truths. This reduces extreme reactions to imagined worst-case scenarios.

Overall, by continually bringing your attention back to the present, mindfulness loosens overthinking's tight grip.

Daily Mindfulness Practices

We've explored how mindfulness helps minimize overthinking by grounding us in the present moment. But how do we actually integrate this state of mindful awareness into daily life? Establishing a regular mindfulness practice is key, and it can look different for everyone. The following exercises can take just a few minutes a day or longer, depending on your preferences and schedule. Just a few minutes a day can make a profound difference over time.

Here are some easy ways to build mindfulness and reduce over-thinking:

- Tune into your breathing—feel your belly rise and fall with each breath.
- Do a body scan—slowly scan your body from head to toe, noticing sensations.
- Take mindful nature walks—focus your senses on sights, sounds, and smells.
- Repeat a mantra—like "I am here now."
- Observe your thoughts as they arise and pass through your mind. Notice them without judgment or attachment, and imagine them floating by like clouds in the sky. As you witness the thoughts coming and going, you'll begin to recognize that you are not your thoughts, only the observer of your thoughts. This realization can help create a sense of detachment and perspective, allowing you to let go of rumination and overthinking more easily.

The key is not to latch onto thoughts but just let them drift on by. This mindful detachment from worries and obsession about the future is powerful. Give it a try!

Solution #2: Thought Challenging

If repetitive worrying has your mind spinning, thought challenging can help you regain control. By identifying and disputing distorted thought patterns driving your worries, this strategy helps shrink unhelpful thoughts down to size.

What Is Thought Challenging?

Thought challenging involves spotting worried thoughts that fuel anxiety, analyzing if they're accurate, and replacing them with balanced perspectives. Often called "distorted thoughts," these tend to amplify apprehension and tension.

Thought challenging starts by pinpointing distorted thoughts. Then, you reframe them to align better with reality. For example, instead of thinking, *I'll definitely mess up this presentation and be humiliated*, you might reframe it as, "I've gotten nervous before presentations but ended up doing fine. If I mess up a bit, it's not catastrophic." The goal is to develop fairer perspectives that keep you grounded.

Common Distorted Thought Patterns

Our minds often play tricks on us, skewing situations negatively. These exaggerated thought patterns are called "cognitive distortions"—and recognizing them helps us challenge anxious, worried thinking. Catching distortions quickly prevents them from fueling storms of overthinking.

To start restructuring imbalanced thinking, it helps to recognize common distorted thought patterns first, like:

- black-or-white thinking—only seeing extreme outcomes with no middle ground
- catastrophizing—assuming the worst-case scenario will for sure happen
- overgeneralization—believing one negative experience reflects an overall pattern
- emotional reasoning—basing conclusions only on feelings rather than facts

Catching and reframing distorted thoughts helps halt them in their tracks.

How to Challenge Thoughts

Once we identify our own characteristic distorted thoughts fueling overthinking, we can start challenging them. This simply means questioning their validity, finding more balanced perspectives, and ultimately quieting our worried inner voice.

To put thought challenging into action:

1. Identify worried, anxious thoughts and the distortions they demonstrate
2. Gather factual evidence against the distortions
3. Develop balanced responses aligned with reality
4. Repeat these new thoughts until they stick

For example, the thought *My friends didn't invite me out; they must not like me* shows emotional reasoning and overgeneralization. We would find evidence that this isn't totally true, like times when they included us. Our balanced response might be *Sometimes friends don't include me but often still want to spend time together.*

With practice, thought challenging retrains the brain's pathways away from exaggeration and toward clarity. Peace of mind can follow!

Solution #3: Distractions, Productivity, and Socializing

When overthinking gets intense, it often helps to shift your focus. Healthy distractions, staying productive, and social connections can help divert your mind from going in worried circles. Let's explore easy tips in each area:

Healthy Distractions

We all need a mental break sometimes from anxious thoughts spiraling out of control. Healthy distractions can provide that mental space and relief. By fully immersing our senses in an enjoyable activity, we halt the momentum of worries, letting them naturally fade into the background. Even a short distraction can help hit the reset button so we return with a clearer perspective.

It's fine to distract your mind briefly from distressing thoughts through

- reading an engrossing novel
- doing a puzzle or playing a game
- watching light-hearted shows
- listening to upbeat music
- going for a run or baking treats

Aim for distractions that fully capture your attention and lift your mood. This mental break can reboot your mind, letting worried thoughts naturally fade.

Staying Productive

Overthinking loves to flood in and occupy any mental space left unattended. An effective solution? Staying actively productive. By immersing yourself in constructive tasks and goals, you prevent unhelpful thoughts from monopolizing your mind. Achieving even small wins reinforces a sense of control and confidence to handle worries that eventually resurface with greater clarity.

Keep your momentum going by

- making to-do lists
- breaking big tasks into small steps
- rewarding progress to stay motivated
- scheduling activities to fill the time

Focusing your mental energy on productive tasks prevents over-thinking from filling the space. Achieving goals boosts confidence to tackle worries that resurface later with clarity.

Increase Your Socialization

Humans are social creatures at our core. During times of emotional turmoil like unrelenting overthinking, the support of caring connections can make all the difference. By voicing your inner worries to close friends and family, their encouragement and reassurance help diminish anxious thoughts' power over time. Even just spending an enjoyable time interacting with loved ones redirects your attention in a positive way.

Plan social activities like

- video chats to catch up with friends
- sharing coffee or meals together
- exercising alongside others
- attending social events virtually or locally

Meaningful connection is healing. Voice concerns openly to loved ones offering non-judgmental ears. Their support helps put anxious thoughts in perspective so they lose intensity over time.

The key is recognizing when overthinking starts hijacking your mind. Once you notice worried thoughts spinning, try shifting gears to any distraction, task, or person that can halt the mental loop and restore balance.

Exercise: Overthinking Trap

The goal of this written exercise is to help identify common over-thinking thought patterns you experience along with the situational triggers that tend to set them in motion. Bringing awareness to these thought traps is the first step in dismantling overthinking tendencies long term.

Let's get started:

Reflect on the last 2–3 times you notice yourself falling into obsessive, worrying thought spirals. These could be at night while trying to fall asleep, during work on challenging projects, in your relationships after disagreements, and so on. Any situation that hooks your mind into a whirling mental tunnel about possible negative outcomes.

Next, for each identified overthinking experience, document the following on a piece of paper, your phone, or a journal:

- What was the situation or trigger preceding the beginning of the thought spiral?
- What specific thoughts or fearful predictions did the overthinking episode revolve around?
- Were there themes or common distortions—like catastrophizing or black-or-white thinking—you tended to indulge around this topic?
- How much time did you spend overanalyzing before catching and redirecting yourself?
- On a 1–10 scale, how disruptive was this bout of overthinking to your productivity and inner peace?

Lastly, based on your observations from these documented over-thinking traps, summarize

- the most common triggers sending you into overthinking
- the top 3–5 thought distortion patterns you default to (ex. blowing things out proportion, imagining only worst-case outcomes, etc.)
- initial ideas for how to catch and combat overthinking when these known triggers and distortions are next activated

Use these revelations of your characteristic thought traps to fuel your motivation and strategy for short-circuiting overthinking going forward! Recognizing our own repeated sticky mental web patterns is illuminating for ultimately changing their trajectory toward wisdom and emotional freedom.

Wrapping Up...

In this first step forward, we've gained skills to stop obsessive worrying and take control of runaway thoughts. We're no longer trapped in tiring mental loops. Now, we can catch anxious thoughts before they spiral and intentionally shift our focus to clarity instead.

We've covered easy yet powerful techniques, including:

- mindfulness practices to ground us in the present
- thought challenging to dispute exaggerated, worried thinking
- helpful coping ideas like healthy distractions and social support

Learning to hit the brakes on a spinning mind paves the way to building real mental strength. By developing internal resilience first, we're better equipped to handle external storms down the road.

Now that we've conquered overthinking's maze, we'll learn how to master stress next. In the next chapter, we'll unlock secrets to responding skillfully to daily pressures and safeguarding our peace of mind. Armed with coping strategies, we'll keep strengthening our mental muscles for any challenge.

Case Study: Amara

Amara's mind had always tended to spiral into imagining worst-case scenarios ever since she was little. As a kid, her anxious thoughts often focused on family members being hurt or her life feeling unstable from moving a lot. As an adult, she channeled this overthinking tendency into excelling at her finance job, planning for every possible bad outcome in her projects.

At first, Amara's constant worrying brought promotions at work for her thorough planning. But over time, the strain of constant overthinking started impacting her health. She developed insomnia, migraines, and an ulcer by age 30. She desperately wished for mental strength to turn off her spinning thoughts when needed.

By chance, one sleepless night, Amara found a book on building mental toughness. She eagerly turned to the chapter called "Stop Overthinking in Its Tracks," hoping to understand and gain control over her exhausting thought spirals.

The chapter explained how brains prone to anxiety get wired to scan for threats on overdrive. Amara learned simple mindfulness practices to catch herself when worries accelerated and purposefully shifted her focus back to the present moment instead. Using a mantra like "I'm here now" helped ground her when anxious thoughts popped up.

Amara also began journaling to get the thoughts out of her head. This, along with techniques to challenge her exaggerated, worst-case obsessions, started retraining her brain toward balance. She posted reminders everywhere saying, "Am I overdoing this?" to trigger herself to rationally reassess scenarios sending her mind spinning.

With practice, Amara caught her mind wandering into anxious mental tunnels much sooner. Hours previously lost in obsessive analysis got redirected into constructive tasks and hobbies that boosted her confidence. Coffee dates and yoga classes with supportive friends eased residual anxiety. For the first time in decades, glimpses of calm appeared, like still waters after an endless storm. From that peace, authentic mental strength grew roots inside Amara.

Amara's overthinking tendencies still arise, but she now has tools to recognize and redirect them effectively. Her story offers hope to anyone locked in exhausting mental loops—we all can retrain our minds toward clarity and tranquility with dedication. By stopping overthinking in its tracks, we reset our path toward inner freedom.

THREE

Step #2—Managing Stress the Right Way

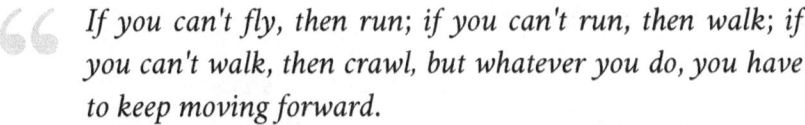 *If you can't fly, then run; if you can't run, then walk; if you can't walk, then crawl, but whatever you do, you have to keep moving forward.*

Martin Luther King Jr.

D r. King's words ring true when it comes to building mental strength and resilience. His quote is a powerful reminder that no matter how tough things get, we have to keep pushing forward, even if it means crawling at times. It's a message that applies to all of us as we navigate the ups and downs of life.

In the last chapter, we took the first step in our journey toward unshakable mental toughness by learning how to quiet the noise of overthinking. It's a skill that takes practice but one that can make a world of difference in our ability to stay focused and grounded in the face of challenges.

Now, we're turning our attention to another major roadblock on the path to mental toughness: stress. Let's face it—stress is a part of life. It's not something we can avoid altogether, but when we let it run rampant, it can take a serious toll on our mental and emotional well-being. It can leave us feeling drained, overwhelmed, and ill-equipped to handle the curve balls that life inevitably throws our way.

But here's the good news: By understanding how stress works and developing a toolbox of strategies to manage it effectively, we can minimize its negative impact and even harness it as a force for growth and resilience.

In this chapter, we're going to take a deep dive into the psychology of stress. We'll explore why we feel it in the first place, how it affects us both mentally and physically, and how we can tell the difference between stress that motivates us to step up our game and stress that tears us down.

But we won't stop at just understanding stress—you'll learn a range of powerful techniques for overcoming it. From simple lifestyle tweaks to relaxation practices to the transformative power of engaging in activities that light you up, you'll come away with a wealth of strategies for building stress resilience and mental toughness.

By the time you finish this chapter, you'll have the knowledge and tools you need to navigate life's challenges with poise, grace, and unwavering mental strength. So, let's dive in and start mastering the art of stress management—your journey to unshakable resilience starts now.

The Problem With Stress

Stress is an unavoidable part of life, affecting people from all walks of life and all age groups. It is a natural response to challenging or threatening situations, triggering a complex cascade of physiological and psychological reactions. While some stress can be beneficial, motivating us to take action and perform at our best, excessive or prolonged stress can have detrimental effects on our mental and physical well-being.

Why We Feel Stress: Psychological Understandings

From a psychological standpoint, stress arises when we perceive a situation as challenging, threatening, or beyond our ability to cope. Common stressors include work deadlines, financial pressures, relationship conflicts, health concerns, and major life changes. Our mind interprets these situations as potential threats to our well-being, triggering the body's stress response.

The stress response is orchestrated by the autonomic nervous system, which activates the "fight-or-flight" response. This ancient survival mechanism prepares the body to face or flee from danger by releasing stress hormones like cortisol and adrenaline. These hormones increase heart rate, blood pressure, and blood sugar levels while diverting energy away from non-essential functions like digestion and immune response.

In the short term, this stress response can enhance focus, alertness, and performance, helping us rise to the challenge at hand. This is often referred to as "good stress" or "eustress." However, when stress becomes chronic or overwhelming, it can take a toll on our mental and physical health. Prolonged exposure to stress hormones can lead to anxiety, depression, impaired cognitive function, weakened immune response, and increased risk of chronic diseases like heart disease and diabetes.

Moreover, our psychological response to stress is shaped by our thoughts, beliefs, and coping strategies. Negative self-talk, catastrophic thinking, and a lack of perceived control can amplify the impact of stress, leading to feelings of helplessness and despair. On the other hand, a positive mindset, effective problem-solving skills, and a strong support system can help buffer the effects of stress and promote resilience.

Understanding the psychological mechanisms of stress is crucial for developing effective stress management strategies. By recognizing the difference between good and bad stress and cultivating a healthy mindset and coping skills, we can harness the benefits of stress while minimizing its negative impact on our well-being.

Common Stressors

In today's fast-paced world, stress can stem from a wide range of sources. Some of the most common stressors include:

- **Work-related stress:** Job demands, long hours, tight deadlines, high-pressure environments, job insecurity, and conflicts with coworkers or supervisors can all contribute to work-related stress.
- **Financial stress:** Money worries, such as debt, bills, unexpected expenses, and financial instability, are a significant source of stress for many people.
- **Relationship stress:** Conflicts with partners, family members, or friends, as well as the stress of caregiving responsibilities or the loss of a loved one, can take a heavy emotional toll.
- **Health-related stress:** Chronic illnesses, injuries, or health scares can be highly stressful, as can the pressure to maintain a healthy lifestyle in the face of busy schedules and competing demands.

- **Major life changes:** Significant life transitions, such as moving, getting married, having a baby, or changing careers, can be exciting but also stressful as they require adaptation and adjustment.
- **Environmental stress:** Factors like noise pollution, traffic, crowding, and climate change can contribute to stress, particularly for those living in urban areas.
- **Social and political stress:** Social pressures, discrimination, and political tensions can be a source of stress, particularly for marginalized or disadvantaged groups.
- **Technology-related stress:** The constant connectivity and information overload of the digital age can lead to "technostress," as well as the stress of managing online relationships and social media pressures.

While these stressors are common, it's important to recognize that stress is a highly individual experience. What may be stressful for one person may not be for another, depending on factors like personality, coping skills, and life circumstances. By identifying our own unique stressors and developing personalized stress management strategies, we can better navigate the challenges of modern life and maintain our well-being in the face of stress.

Good vs. Bad Stress

Not all stress is created equal. While we often think of stress as a negative force, some stress can actually be beneficial. Psychologists often distinguish between "good stress" (also known as "eustress") and "bad stress" (or "distress").

Good stress is the kind of stress that energizes and motivates us. It's the excitement we feel when taking on a new challenge, the adrenaline rush of a looming deadline, or the butterflies in our stomachs before a big presentation. This type of stress can enhance our focus, creativity, and performance, pushing us to grow and achieve our goals. Good stress is typically short-lived and within our coping abilities.

Examples of good stress include:

- starting a new job or taking on a challenging project
- preparing for a wedding or other significant life event
- engaging in physical exercise or competition
- stepping outside of your comfort zone to learn a new skill

In contrast, bad stress is the kind of stress that overwhelms us and exceeds our ability to cope. It's the feeling of being buried under a mountain of responsibilities, the anxiety of a toxic work environment, or the exhaustion of caring for a chronically ill loved one. Bad stress is often chronic, meaning it persists over an extended period, and can lead to a host of negative physical and mental health outcomes.

Examples of bad stress include:

- enduring an abusive relationship
- struggling with chronic financial insecurity
- dealing with the aftermath of a traumatic event

The key difference between good and bad stress lies in our perception and response. Good stress feels manageable and meaningful, while bad stress feels overwhelming and beyond our control. Moreover, what may be good stress for one person may be bad stress for another, depending on individual resilience and coping skills.

In order to harness the benefits of good stress while minimizing the impact of bad stress, it's essential to develop effective stress management techniques. This may include practices like exercise, time management, and seeking support when needed. By learning to distinguish between good and bad stress and responding accordingly, we can cultivate a healthy relationship with stress that allows us to thrive in the face of life's challenges.

Solution #1: Lifestyle Changes

Making simple lifestyle changes can have a profound impact on reducing stress and building mental toughness. By focusing on three key areas—diet, exercise, and sleep—you can create a solid foundation for managing stress effectively.

Diet

What you eat can significantly influence your stress levels and overall mental well-being. A healthy, balanced diet rich in whole foods, fruits, vegetables, lean proteins, and healthy fats can help regulate mood, improve energy levels, and support brain function.

When you're stressed, your body releases cortisol, a hormone that can trigger cravings for high-fat, high-sugar foods. While these foods may provide temporary comfort, they can ultimately lead to feelings of guilt, sluggishness, and increased stress. By making healthier food choices, you can help break this cycle and support your body's natural stress-fighting abilities.

To make better dietary choices for stress management:

- **Incorporate stress-reducing foods:** Certain foods, such as dark chocolate, nuts, seeds, fatty fish, and avocados, contain nutrients that can help reduce stress and promote relaxation. For example, dark chocolate is rich in magnesium, which can help regulate cortisol levels, while fatty fish like salmon and tuna are high in omega-3 fatty acids, which have been shown to reduce inflammation and support brain health.

- **Limit processed and sugary foods:** These foods can cause blood sugar spikes and crashes, leading to increased stress and anxiety. They also tend to be low in nutrients and high in empty calories, which can contribute to feelings of fatigue and irritability. Instead, opt for whole, unprocessed foods that provide sustained energy and essential vitamins and minerals.

- **Stay hydrated:** Dehydration can exacerbate feelings of stress and fatigue, so aim to drink plenty of water throughout the day. Even mild dehydration can lead to headaches, difficulty concentrating, and mood changes. Keep a water bottle with you and sip regularly, especially during stressful situations.

- **Practice mindful eating:** Take the time to sit down and enjoy your meals without distractions, paying attention to the flavors, textures, and sensations of your food. Mindful eating can help you tune in to your body's hunger and fullness cues, reducing the likelihood of stress-related overeating. It also allows you to savor and appreciate your food, turning mealtime into a relaxing and enjoyable experience.

- **Plan ahead:** Stress can often lead to impulsive food choices, so it's helpful to plan your meals and snacks in advance. Prepare healthy options like cut vegetables, hummus, or trail mix to have on hand when cravings strike. When you have a busy day ahead, pack a nutritious lunch and snacks to avoid relying on fast food or vending machines.

Exercise

Regular physical activity is one of the most effective ways to combat stress and build mental toughness. Exercise releases endorphins, the body's natural mood boosters, and helps reduce stress hormones like cortisol. It also improves sleep quality, boosts self-confidence, and provides a healthy outlet for frustration and anxiety.

When you exercise, your body undergoes physiological changes that help reduce stress and improve overall well-being. Your heart rate increases, your breathing deepens, and your muscles work harder, all of which can help release tension and improve circulation. Over time, regular exercise can also help you build resilience to stress, making it easier to cope with challenging situations.

To incorporate exercise into your stress management routine:

- **Find activities you enjoy:** Whether it's walking, swimming, dancing, or playing a sport, choose exercises that you find enjoyable and sustainable. When you look forward to your workouts, you're more likely to stick with them long-term. Experiment with different activities until you find ones that resonate with you.
- **Start small:** If you're new to exercise, begin with just a few minutes a day and gradually increase the duration and intensity over time. Even a short, 10-minute walk can provide stress-reducing benefits.
- **Make it a habit:** Consistency is key when it comes to reaping the stress-reducing benefits of exercise. Aim to

incorporate physical activity into your daily routine, even if it's just a short walk during your lunch break. Schedule your workouts like you would any other important appointment, and treat them as non-negotiable self-care time.

- **Try stress-specific exercises:** Certain activities, such as yoga, tai chi, and Qigong, are particularly effective for reducing stress and promoting relaxation. These practices combine physical movement with deep breathing and meditation, helping to calm the mind and release tension in the body. Consider attending a class or following along with a video to learn proper technique and form.

- **Get outside:** Exercising in nature can provide additional stress-reducing benefits. Exposure to greenery, fresh air, and natural light can help improve mood, reduce anxiety, and promote a sense of calm. Take a hike, go for a bike ride, or simply do your regular workout in a nearby park or beach.

Sleep

Getting enough quality sleep is essential for managing stress and maintaining mental toughness. Sleep deprivation can exacerbate feelings of stress, anxiety, and irritability while also impairing cognitive function and decision-making skills.

During sleep, your body undergoes important restorative processes, including the release of growth hormones, tissue repair, and memory consolidation. Lack of sleep can disrupt these processes, leading to increased inflammation, weakened immune function, and impaired emotional regulation. Over time, chronic sleep deprivation can take a serious toll on both physical and mental health.

Steps to improve your sleep so you can better manage stress include:

- **Establish a consistent sleep schedule:** Go to bed and wake up at the same time to establish a strong internal clock pattern. Consistency is key, as even small variations in sleep timing can disrupt your sleep quality.
- **Create a relaxing bedtime routine:** Develop a calming pre-sleep ritual, such as taking a warm bath, reading a book, or practicing relaxation techniques like deep breathing or meditation. Having rituals tells your body that it's time to start winding down. Avoid stimulating activities like watching TV or scrolling through social media, as these can make it harder to fall asleep.
- **Optimize your sleep environment:** Ensure your bedroom is cool, quiet, and dark, and invest in a comfortable mattress and pillows. Use earplugs or a white noise machine to block out disruptive sounds, and consider using blackout curtains or an eye mask to eliminate light pollution. Keep your bedroom tidy and clutter-free to promote a sense of calm and relaxation.
- **Limit screen time before bed:** The blue light emitted by electronic devices can interfere with your body's natural sleep-wake cycle, so try to avoid screens for at least an hour before bedtime. If you must use a device, consider using blue light-blocking glasses or installing a blue light filter app to reduce your exposure.
- **Avoid caffeine and alcohol close to bedtime:** These substances can disrupt sleep quality and make it harder to fall asleep. Caffeine can stay in your system for up to eight hours, so it's best to avoid it after lunchtime. While alcohol may initially make you feel drowsy, it can interfere with

deep, restorative sleep and cause middle-of-the-night awakenings.

- **Practice good sleep hygiene:** In addition to the above tips, there are several other habits that can promote better sleep. Avoid large meals, intense exercise, and stressful activities close to bedtime. Keep your bedroom temperature cool, around 60–67°F (15–19°C). If you can't fall asleep within 20–30 minutes, get out of bed and do a calming activity until you feel sleepy.

By making these lifestyle changes and prioritizing diet, exercise, and sleep, you can significantly reduce your stress levels, build mental toughness, and improve your overall well-being. Remember that change takes time, and it's okay to start small and gradually build upon your progress. Be patient with yourself, celebrate your successes, and don't hesitate to seek support from friends, family, or a mental health professional if needed.

Solution #2: Relaxation Techniques

Incorporating relaxation techniques, such as breathing exercises and meditation, into your daily routine can be a powerful way to manage stress and promote a sense of calm and well-being. These practices help activate the body's natural relaxation response, reducing stress hormones, lowering blood pressure, and promoting feelings of peace and tranquility.

Breathing

Breathing exercises are a simple yet effective way to reduce stress and anxiety. When you're stressed, your breathing tends to become shallow and rapid, which can exacerbate feelings of tension and unease. By consciously slowing down and deepening your breath, you can signal to your body that it's time to relax and unwind.

Here are three breathing techniques to try:

- **Diaphragmatic breathing:** The key here is to focus on breathing deeply into your diaphragm, rather than taking shallow breaths into your chest. To do this, place one hand on your chest and the other on your belly. As you inhale slowly through your nose, you should feel your belly rise like a balloon filling with air. Then, exhale slowly through pursed lips, as if you're blowing out a candle, and feel your belly fall. Aim for 5-10 breaths like this, and you'll be amazed at how much calmer you feel.
- **4-7-8 breathing:** Find a comfortable seated position with your back straight, and place the tip of your tongue against the ridge behind your upper front teeth. Start by exhaling completely through your mouth, making a "whoosh" sound. Then, close your mouth and quietly inhale through your nose for a count of 4. Hold that breath for a count of 7, and then exhale completely through your mouth (making that "whoosh" sound again) for a count of 8. Repeat this cycle 3–4 times, and feel your worries start to melt away.
- **Alternate nostril breathing:** This yogic technique is said to help balance the left and right hemispheres of the brain, promoting relaxation and mental clarity. To try it, sit comfortably with your back straight and rest your left hand on your lap. Use your right thumb to gently close your right nostril, and take a deep breath in through your left nostril. Then, close your left nostril with your ring finger, release your thumb from your right nostril, and exhale through your right nostril. Now, inhale through

your right nostril, close it with your thumb, release your ring finger from your left nostril, and exhale through your left nostril. Repeat this pattern for 5-10 cycles, and notice how much more centered and focused you feel.

Meditation

Meditation is a powerful tool for reducing stress, improving focus, and cultivating a sense of inner peace. By training your mind to be present and non-judgmental, you can learn to observe your thoughts and emotions without getting caught up in them, reducing their power to cause stress and anxiety.

Here are two guided meditations to try:

- **Body scan meditation:** This meditation involves systematically focusing on each part of your body, from your toes to your head, bringing awareness to any sensations or tension you may feel. Lie down or sit comfortably with your eyes closed. Take a few deep breaths, allowing your body to settle. Starting with your toes, bring your attention to any sensations you feel in that part of your body. If you notice any tension, imagine your breath flowing into that area, releasing and relaxing it. Slowly move your attention up your body, focusing on each part in turn until you reach the top of your head. Allow yourself to rest in a state of relaxed awareness for a few moments before gently opening your eyes.
- **Loving-kindness meditation:** This meditation involves cultivating feelings of love, compassion, and goodwill toward yourself and others. Sit comfortably with your eyes closed. Take a few deep breaths, allowing your body to settle. Bring to mind someone you love and appreciate,

and silently repeat the following phrases: "May you be happy. May you be healthy. May you be safe. May you live with ease." Next, bring to mind someone you feel neutral toward, and repeat the phrases. Then, bring to mind someone you find challenging, and repeat the phrases. Finally, extend these feelings of loving-kindness to all beings everywhere, silently repeating: "May all beings be happy. May all beings be healthy. May all beings be safe. May all beings live with ease."

Remember, the key to benefiting from relaxation techniques is consistency. Aim to practice your chosen techniques for at least 5–10 minutes a day, gradually increasing the duration as you become more comfortable. It may feel challenging at first, but with regular practice, you'll find it easier to quiet your mind and tap into a sense of inner calm.

In addition to breathing exercises and meditation, there are many other relaxation techniques to explore, such as progressive muscle relaxation, visualization, and yoga. Experiment with different techniques to find what works best for you, and don't hesitate to seek guidance from a qualified instructor or therapist if needed.

By incorporating relaxation techniques into your daily routine, you can cultivate a greater sense of resilience and equanimity in the face of life's challenges. These practices can help you stay grounded, focused, and calm, even in the midst of stress and uncertainty. With regular practice, you'll develop a powerful set of tools for managing stress, improving your well-being, and enhancing your overall quality of life.

Solution #3: Do What You Love

Engaging in hobbies and activities that bring you joy and fulfill-ment can be a powerful way to reduce stress, improve your mental well-being, and build mental toughness. When you immerse your-self in an activity you love, you create a sense of flow and mindful-ness that can help you forget about your worries and stressors, even if only for a little while.

How Hobbies Improve Stress Levels

Hobbies provide a much-needed break from the demands and pressures of daily life, allowing you to recharge your batteries and return to your responsibilities with renewed energy and focus. When you engage in an activity you enjoy, your body releases endorphins, the natural mood-boosting chemicals that promote feelings of happiness and well-being.

In addition to providing a sense of pleasure and accomplishment, hobbies can also help you develop new skills, build social connec-tions, and cultivate a sense of purpose and meaning. All of these factors can contribute to greater resilience and mental toughness in the face of stress and adversity.

Some of the ways hobbies can improve stress levels include:

- **Providing a sense of control:** When you engage in a hobby, you have the power to choose what you do and how you do it. This sense of control can be especially valuable during times of stress, when many aspects of life may feel outside of your control.
- **Promoting mindfulness:** Hobbies that require focus and concentration, such as painting, gardening, or playing an instrument, can help you cultivate a sense of mindfulness

and presence. By immersing yourself in the task at hand, you can quiet your mind and find relief from stress and worry.

- **Boosting self-esteem:** As you develop new skills and achieve goals related to your hobby, you'll likely experience a sense of pride and accomplishment. This can help boost your self-esteem and confidence, making you feel more capable of handling life's challenges.
- **Providing social support:** Many hobbies involve interacting with others who share your interests, whether through clubs, classes, or online communities. These social connections can provide a valuable source of support and camaraderie during times of stress.

Best Hobbies for Stress Relief

The best hobby for stress relief is one that you genuinely enjoy and look forward to. That said, certain types of hobbies may be particularly beneficial for reducing stress and promoting relaxation. Here are a few ideas:

- **Creative pursuits:** Engaging in creative activities, such as drawing, painting, writing, or crafting, can be a powerful way to express your emotions, process stress, and find a sense of calm and focus. These hobbies allow you to enter a state of flow, where you become fully absorbed in the task at hand and forget about your worries.
- **Physical activities:** Exercise is a well-known stress reliever, and hobbies that involve physical activity can be especially beneficial. Whether it's dancing, hiking, cycling, or playing a sport, moving your body can help release tension, boost your mood, and improve your overall sense of well-being.

- **Gardening and nature-based activities:** Spending time in nature has been shown to reduce stress, improve mood, and promote feelings of peace and tranquility. Hobbies such as gardening, birdwatching, or nature photography can help you connect with the natural world and find a sense of grounding and perspective.
- **Learning and intellectual pursuits:** Engaging in hobbies that challenge your mind, such as reading, learning a new language, or playing chess, can help you stay mentally sharp and engaged. These activities provide a sense of accomplishment and can help you maintain a positive outlook even during difficult times.

Remember, the key to using hobbies for stress relief is to choose activities that you genuinely enjoy and that fit your lifestyle and preferences. Don't be afraid to try new things and experiment until you find hobbies that resonate with you.

By making time for hobbies and activities that bring you joy and fulfillment, you can create a powerful buffer against stress and build greater mental toughness and resilience. These practices can help you stay grounded, focused, and positive, even in the face of life's challenges. So, whether it's picking up a paintbrush, lacing up your hiking boots, or rolling out your yoga mat, make sure to prioritize doing what you love as part of your overall stress management strategy.

Wrapping Up...

In this chapter, we took a deep dive into the world of stress management, exploring effective strategies for reducing stress and building mental toughness. By making simple lifestyle changes and incorporating relaxation techniques into your daily routine, you can significantly improve your ability to handle life's challenges with grace and resilience.

We've covered a range of powerful tools, including:

- optimizing your diet, exercise, and sleep habits to create a solid foundation for stress management
- practicing breathing exercises to activate your body's natural relaxation response and promote feelings of calm
- incorporating meditation into your daily routine to cultivate mindfulness, focus, and inner peace
- engaging in activities that you love and bring you joy

Learning to manage stress effectively is a crucial component of developing mental toughness. By taking proactive steps to reduce stress and promote well-being, you'll be better equipped to navigate life's ups and downs with clarity, resilience, and strength.

Now that we've mastered the art of stress management, we'll turn our attention to the power of emotional agility. In the next chapter, we'll explore how developing emotional agility can help you navigate complex feelings, accept and utilize emotions effectively, and further strengthen your mental toughness. Get ready to discover the transformative potential of cultivating emotional agility and nurturing your inner resilience.

Case Study: Michael

Meet Michael, a 40-year-old software engineer who thought he had it all figured out when it came to dealing with pressure. He was the guy who always stepped up when deadlines were tight, working long hours and subsisting on a diet of coffee and takeout. He wore his ability to handle stress like a badge of honor.

However, as the years went by and the demands on his time and energy kept piling up, Michael started to feel the cracks in his armor. He was snapping at coworkers, struggling to focus, and feeling like he was constantly running on empty. His once-active lifestyle had fallen by the wayside, replaced by late nights at the office and a growing sense of overwhelm.

It was a wake-up call for Michael when he realized that his "push through it" approach to stress management just wasn't cutting it anymore. He knew he needed to make some changes if he wanted to get his mental well-being back on track.

So, he started small. He began by taking a hard look at his diet and making some simple swaps—more nuts and seeds for snacks, less caffeine, and plenty of water to stay hydrated. He dusted off his old basketball and joined a local league, committing to weekly games as a way to get moving and blow off some steam. He started biking to work, using the morning ride as a chance to clear his head and set a positive tone for the day.

Next, Michael turned his attention to his sleep habits. He created a relaxing bedtime routine, complete with stretching and journaling and invested in a comfortable new mattress and pillows. He also started experimenting with relaxation techniques, like deep breathing and mindfulness meditation, to help calm his racing thoughts and ease feelings of anxiety.

As Michael started to prioritize his physical and mental health, he noticed a shift in his ability to handle stress. He was able to approach challenges at work with a clearer head and a more resilient mindset. His relationships with colleagues and loved ones improved as he learned to communicate more effectively and respond to pressure in a healthier way.

Through this journey, Michael discovered that building mental toughness isn't about burning the candle at both ends or pushing yourself to the brink of exhaustion. It's about developing a toolkit of strategies and habits that allow you to navigate life's inevitable stresses with grace and resilience.

By making simple changes to his lifestyle and incorporating relaxation techniques into his daily routine, Michael was able to transform his relationship with stress and cultivate the mental strength he needed to thrive—both at work and in his personal life.

His story is a powerful reminder that no matter how overwhelming stress may feel in the moment, we all have the power to take control of our well-being and build the mental toughness we need to overcome any obstacle that comes our way.

FOUR

Step #3—Honing Emotional Agility

 Out of suffering have emerged the strongest souls; the most massive characters are seared with scars.

Khalil Gibran

L ife is full of ups and downs, joys and sorrows, triumphs and challenges. No matter how mentally tough or resilient you are, you will inevitably encounter difficult emotions along the way —grief, fear, anger, shame, disappointment. The key to thriving in the face of adversity is not to avoid or suppress these feelings but to develop the agility to face them courageously and use them as fuel for growth.

This is where emotional agility comes in. Emotional agility is the ability to be with your emotions in a healthy way—to acknowledge and accept your inner experiences without being controlled by them. It's about treating your feelings as data to learn from rather than directives you must blindly obey. With emotional agility, you cultivate the flexibility and resilience to deal with life's challenges and changes with grace, clarity, and purposeful action.

In this chapter, you'll learn the mindsets and skills of emotional agility. You'll discover how to be aware of your emotions without being swept away by them, question your thoughts and assumptions, and choose intentional responses aligned with your values. No longer will you be at the mercy of knee-jerk reactions or emotional storms. Instead, you'll be able to navigate your inner world like a skilled captain at the helm of a ship—aware of the changing tides and weather but steering your course with wisdom and intention.

Emotional agility is a superpower that enables you to extract the lessons and growth opportunities from any adversity. When you can acknowledge the full depths of your emotional world with honesty and self-compassion, you liberate yourself from suffering and struggle. You gain access to your inner reserves of clarity, creativity and coping. Challenges become chances to evolve and emotions become allies on the path to meaning and mastery.

Get ready to radically transform your relationship with your emotions and upgrade your mental toughness with the skills of emotional agility. By the end of this chapter, you'll have potent tools and techniques to navigate the inevitable ups and downs of life with unwavering inner strength and flexibility. True freedom, fulfillment and resilience await as you learn to embrace the power of emotional agility.

What Is Emotional Agility?

Emotional agility is the ability to experience your thoughts, emotions, and events in a way that doesn't drive you in negative directions but instead encourages you to reveal the best of yourself. Rather than ignoring difficult emotions or getting swept away by them, emotional agility is about facing your inner experiences with courage and compassion and then choosing how to move forward intentionally in line with your values and goals.

Picture a tree in the midst of a storm, battered by heavy winds and rain. Its branches sway and bend with the gusts, but ultimately, the tree remains rooted and grounded. It adapts to the changing conditions without snapping or toppling over. This is what emotional agility looks like—having the flexibility, strength, and resilience to navigate life's ups and downs while staying true to yourself and what matters most to you.

When you cultivate emotional agility, you allow yourself to feel the full range of emotions, even the unpleasant ones, without getting hooked by them. You acknowledge and accept what you're feeling, understand where those feelings are coming from, and then proactively choose how to respond rather than reacting on autopilot. You maintain clarity about your deepest priorities so you can align your actions with your values, even when faced with stress or adversity.

With emotional agility, you learn to experience emotions as transient states that come and go, like clouds passing across the sky. Instead of identifying with your feelings or viewing them as permanent reflections of who you are, you recognize them as temporary experiences to learn from as you continue moving forward purposefully. Emotional agility empowers you to be courageous, vulnerable, and resilient as you navigate the inevitable complexities of life and work. It frees you up to engage fully, take risks, and thrive.

Benefits of Emotional Agility

Cultivating emotional agility provides a multitude of powerful benefits that can transform your life, work, and relationships for the better. When you develop the skills to mindfully navigate your inner world, you open the door to greater resilience, authenticity, and effectiveness.

One of the key advantages of emotional agility is improved psychological health and well-being. By learning to face and accept the full range of your emotions, you build distress tolerance and reduce emotional suffering. You're less likely to get trapped in toxic cycles of rumination, blame, or avoidance. This frees up mental and emotional bandwidth so you can focus on what truly matters.

Emotional agility also fosters stronger, more authentic relationships. When you can bravely acknowledge your own feelings and hold space for others' emotions, you create the conditions for genuine intimacy and connection. You communicate more openly and honestly, leading to greater understanding and trust. You're also better equipped to navigate conflicts or difficult conversations with grace and skill.

In the workplace, emotional agility is a key driver of success, particularly in fast-paced, high-pressure, or ambiguous environments. Leaders and employees who can deftly manage their own emotions are more adaptable, proactive, and solution-focused. They bounce back quicker from setbacks, take more calculated risks, and perform better under stress. Emotional agility enables you to communicate a compelling vision, have challenging conversations, and unite and inspire others.

Another powerful benefit of emotional agility is greater self-knowledge, personal growth, and overall life satisfaction. By mindfully observing your thought patterns and emotional habits, you develop keener self-awareness and insight. This empowers you to consciously choose behaviors and responses that are adaptive and aligned with your values. Over time, you learn to author your life story and shape your experiences in a way that is meaningful and fulfilling to you.

Ultimately, emotional agility liberates you from being controlled by your thoughts, feelings, and circumstances. It provides a path to realize your fullest potential and thrive, not just in the absence of challenge but in the very midst of it. When you develop a more agile, resilient inner world, your outer world transforms in remarkable ways.

Solution #1: Logical and Critical Thinking

One of the most effective ways to build emotional agility and mental toughness is to harness the power of logical and critical thinking. When you learn to analyze situations objectively, question assumptions, and reason through problems systematically, you gain greater control over your mind and emotions. Let's explore what logical and critical thinking entails and how to cultivate these invaluable skills.

What Is Critical Thinking?

At its core, critical thinking is the ability to analyze information objectively and make a reasoned judgment. It involves looking at situations from all angles, evaluating evidence and arguments rationally, and reaching well-founded conclusions. Critical thinkers ask probing questions, challenge assumptions, and resist jumping to conclusions based on emotions or preconceived notions.

Some key traits of critical thinking include:

- questioning evidence and assumptions
- analyzing connections and patterns objectively
- reasoning through logic and weighing probabilities
- recognizing and avoiding cognitive biases
- considering alternate possibilities and perspectives
- reaching evidence-based conclusions
- communicating rationally to explain thinking

Critical thinking enables you to navigate complex situations with greater mental clarity, solve problems more effectively, and make sounder decisions aligned with your goals. When you approach challenges as a critical thinker, you build mental resilience to stay level-headed even in emotionally charged situations.

Thinking With Reason

Logical thinking is a critical component of developing emotional agility. It involves analyzing cause-and-effect relationships, recognizing patterns, and understanding the likely outcomes of different choices. By gathering relevant facts and evidence, questioning assumptions, and considering probabilities, you can draw well-founded conclusions based on reasoning rather than emotional reactivity.

To strengthen your logical thinking skills, start by cultivating a habit of gathering relevant information and data to inform your reasoning. This may include past experiences, concrete evidence, and expert insights. Next, challenge your preconceived notions and confirm that you're working with facts rather than unexamined beliefs. Look for patterns, connections, and cause-and-effect relationships between events to understand how they impact each other.

When faced with a decision or challenge, consider the probable outcomes of different actions by reasoning through "if-then" logic. Avoid the temptation to oversimplify complex issues or overlook nuance by resisting generalizations and black-and-white thinking. Instead, strive to reach reasonable conclusions that are supported by the available facts and evidence.

By routinely practicing logical thinking, you train your mind to respond rationally to stressful situations rather than getting hijacked by volatile emotions. This enables you to approach problems with mental clarity and identify optimal solutions, even in the face of adversity.

The Importance of Critical and Logical Thinking

Developing critical and logical thinking skills is essential for navigating life's challenges with emotional agility. By questioning initial assumptions, gathering relevant data, exploring alternative perspectives, and analyzing cause-and-effect relationships, you can respond intentionally rather than reactively to stressful situations.

One key aspect of critical thinking is checking for cognitive distortions—such as catastrophizing, overgeneralizing, or discounting positives—that can skew your perception of a situation. By objectively examining your thoughts and feelings, you can identify any irrational or unproductive patterns and replace them with more balanced, realistic thinking.

Logical thinking enables you to reason through possible solutions and choose a course of action most likely to generate positive outcomes. By weighing the probable consequences of different choices and reaching an objective conclusion aligned with your goals and values, you can respond effectively to any challenge.

With practice, critical and logical thinking skills become habitual, allowing you to approach stressful situations with mental toughness and resilience. By integrating lessons learned from past experiences, you continually refine your ability to navigate life's obstacles with emotional agility and grace. Ultimately, developing a rational, grounded mindset empowers you to thrive in the face of adversity and maintain emotional equilibrium, even in the most challenging circumstances.

Solution #2: Emotional Awareness

Another critical component of developing emotional agility and mental toughness is cultivating emotional awareness. When you can accurately identify and understand your own emotions, you gain valuable insight into your inner world. This self-knowledge becomes a powerful tool for managing your thoughts, feelings, and reactions more effectively.

Understanding Emotional Awareness

Emotional awareness is the ability to recognize and understand your own emotions as they occur. It involves paying attention to your inner experiences, including physical sensations, thoughts, and feelings. With high emotional awareness, you can accurately identify and name your emotions, understand their sources, and recognize how they impact your behaviors and decisions.

Some key aspects of emotional awareness include:

- noticing and naming your emotions accurately

- identifying the triggers or sources of your feelings
- recognizing how emotions impact your thoughts and behaviors
- understanding the nuances and complexities of emotions
- linking current emotions to past experiences and patterns
- anticipating potential emotional reactions to situations

When you cultivate emotional awareness, you're better able to manage your inner world proactively. You can spot emotional triggers, anticipate challenging situations, and take steps to regulate your reactions. Emotional awareness allows you to respond intentionally rather than getting derailed by unexpected or overwhelming feelings.

Tips for Emotional Awareness

Building emotional awareness is an ongoing practice that gets easier over time. Use these tips to tune into your inner world and strengthen your emotional agility:

- **Pay attention to physical sensations.** Notice changes in your body, like tightness in your chest or butterflies in your stomach, as clues to underlying emotions.
- **Identify and name your feelings specifically.** Go beyond generic labels like "good" or "bad" to pinpoint precise emotions like excited, disappointed, proud, or anxious.
- **Notice your emotional triggers.** Recognize the situations, people, or events that tend to spark specific feelings for you.
- **Explore the root causes of your reactions.** Look beneath surface-level emotions to understand the core fears, beliefs, or past experiences driving your feelings.

- **Keep an emotions journal.** Writing about your daily emotional experiences helps you process feelings and spot recurring patterns over time.
- **Tune into your self-talk.** Notice the inner dialogue impacting your emotions, like harsh self-criticism or catastrophic predictions.
- **Practice mindfulness.** Develop present-moment awareness of your thoughts and feelings through practices like meditation or deep breathing.
- **Cultivate curiosity and self-compassion.** Approach your emotions with openness and kindness rather than self-judgment.

As you build emotional awareness, you start to recognize your unique patterns of thoughts, feelings, and reactions. You discover the emotional strengths and skills that help you navigate challenges effectively, like the ability to bounce back after setbacks or stay calm under pressure. You also identify the emotional triggers or tendencies that undermine your resilience and mental toughness, like a habit of worrying or a fear of failure.

With this self-knowledge, you can focus on leveraging your emotional strengths and developing the agility skills you need to thrive. Emotional awareness becomes the foundation for effectively managing your inner world. You learn to catch problematic thoughts or emotional reactions early, implement proactive coping strategies, and consciously choose responses that align with your values and goals.

By developing emotional awareness, you build the mental toughness and flexibility to navigate life's ups and downs masterfully. You face the full depths of your emotional world with honesty, clarity, and self-compassion. Challenges become opportunities for growth and learning. No matter what arises, you have the self-knowledge and emotional agility to choose intentional responses that keep you grounded, centered, and moving forward purposefully.

Solution #3: Bouncing Back With Resilience

Emotional agility and mental toughness are ultimately about resilience—the ability to face adversity, navigate challenges, and bounce back stronger. Resilience is a key theme that we explore in depth in the book *Mastering Emotional Intelligence With Ease*. Readers who have already delved into that resource will find that the concepts and strategies discussed here build upon and complement the resilience skills covered in that book.

In *Mastering Emotional Intelligence With Ease*, we lay the foundation for understanding what resilience is and why it's so critical for emotional well-being. We explore the core components of resilience, such as self-awareness, adaptability, and a growth mindset. The book also provides practical exercises and techniques for developing these resilience skills in daily life.

Building upon that foundational knowledge, the strategies we'll explore in this section focus specifically on how resilience relates to emotional agility and mental toughness. We'll delve into targeted techniques for boosting resilience in the face of challenges and setbacks, such as reframing adversity, cultivating optimism, and practicing self-compassion. We'll also emphasize the power of social support and strong relationships in fostering resilience.

For readers who haven't yet explored *Mastering Emotional Intelligence With Ease*, that book offers a comprehensive look at the science and practice of resilience. You'll gain a deeper under-standing of the psychological factors that contribute to resilience, as well as evidence-based strategies for strengthening your ability to bounce back from setbacks. The book also provides valuable insights into how resilience intersects with other key areas of emotional intelligence, such as self-awareness, empathy, and motivation.

Whether you've already read *Mastering Emotional Intelligence With Ease* or are new to these concepts, the strategies and insights covered in this section will empower you to cultivate the resilience needed to thrive in the face of any challenge. By combining the foundational knowledge from the previous book with the targeted techniques explored here, you'll develop a comprehensive toolkit for navigating life's obstacles with emotional agility, mental tough-ness, and resilience. Let's dive in and explore practical strategies to boost your resilience and leverage the power of social support.

How to be More Resilient

Resilience is like a muscle—it can be strengthened over time with practice and persistence. Use these proven tips and techniques to build your resilience:

- **Reframe challenges as opportunities.** Look for the potential benefits or lessons in difficult situations. Adopt a growth mindset and view obstacles as chances to learn and improve.
- **Focus on what you can control.** When faced with adversity, direct your energy toward what's within your sphere of influence rather than fixating on factors beyond your control.

- **Practice self-care.** Prioritize healthy habits like proper nutrition, regular exercise, quality sleep, and stress management techniques. Taking care of your physical and emotional well-being builds resilience.
- **Cultivate a positive outlook.** Look for the good in situations and people. Practice gratitude, savor joyful moments, and maintain a hopeful perspective about the future.
- **Set realistic goals and take action.** Break challenges down into manageable steps and take consistent action toward your objectives. Celebrate your progress along the way.
- **Learn from setbacks.** When you encounter obstacles or failures, reflect on what you can learn from the experience. Identify areas for improvement and adjust your approach accordingly.
- **Nurture a strong support system.** Surround yourself with positive, supportive people who believe in you. Reach out for help and encouragement when needed.
- **Develop a sense of purpose.** Connect to your core values and life meaning. Pursue activities and goals that energize and inspire you. A strong sense of purpose fuels resilience.

By incorporating these strategies into your life, you train your mind and emotions to be more resilient. You develop the agility and grit to face any challenge head-on, knowing that you have the inner resources to cope effectively and emerge stronger.

Finding Support in Others

One of the most powerful ways to boost resilience is to cultivate a strong support system. Connecting with others provides a vital source of encouragement, guidance, and practical help during tough times. When you have people you can count on, you're better able to weather any storm.

To build a resilient support network:

- **Identify your support squad.** Make a list of the people in your life who are positive, reliable, and encouraging. Consider family, friends, colleagues, mentors, or professionals like counselors or coaches.
- **Nurture your relationships.** Invest time and energy into building strong, healthy connections with your support people. Show up for them during their challenging times, too.
- **Communicate openly and honestly.** Share your struggles, fears, and goals with trusted confidantes. Allow yourself to be vulnerable and ask for help when needed.
- **Seek out role models and mentors.** Connect with people who have navigated challenges similar to your own. Learn from their experiences and insights.
- **Join supportive communities.** Participate in groups or organizations aligned with your values and interests, where you can find a sense of belonging and shared purpose.
- **Offer support to others.** Providing encouragement and assistance to others facing tough times not only helps them but also boosts your own resilience and sense of meaning.

Remember, resilience isn't about facing challenges alone or being completely self-reliant. It's about knowing when to lean on others and being willing to accept support. By surrounding yourself with caring, encouraging people, you create a powerful buffer against life's storms. You're reminded that you aren't alone, that you're valued and believed in.

Ultimately, emotional agility, mental toughness, and resilience are interconnected skills that empower you to face any challenge with confidence and grace. By developing self-awareness, critical thinking abilities, and a supportive network, you cultivate the inner strength to overcome obstacles and create the life you envision. No matter what arises, you trust in your ability to feel your emotions fully, respond intentionally, and continue moving forward with purpose and conviction.

Wrapping Up...

In this chapter, we explored emotional agility, uncovering its impact on cultivating mental toughness and resilience. By honing the skills to consciously and intentionally navigate your emotional landscape, you gain the flexibility and inner strength to thrive in the face of any challenge.

Throughout this chapter, we've covered essential strategies for honing our emotional agility, including:

- Harnessing logical and critical thinking, analyzing situations objectively, questioning assumptions, reasoning through problems systematically, and reaching evidence-based conclusions before reacting emotionally.
- Cultivating emotional awareness, tuning into your inner world, accurately identifying and understanding your emotions, recognizing triggers and patterns, and exploring the root causes and impacts of your feelings.
- Building resilience, reframing challenges as opportunities, focusing on what you can control, cultivating a positive outlook, learning from setbacks, and leaning on a strong support system to bounce back stronger from adversity.

Emotional agility is a critical component of mental toughness, empowering you to harness the insights and energy of your emotions rather than being controlled by them. By developing self-mastery and emotional intelligence, you'll be equipped to navigate change, uncertainty, and adversity with unwavering inner calm and resolve.

As we continue our journey toward unbreakable mental strength, the next chapter will take us into the realm of authentic confidence and self-assuredness. We'll explore powerful strategies for rewriting limiting beliefs, upgrading your identity, and boldly stepping into your full potential. Get ready to experience the unstoppable force of true confidence combined with emotional agility as you unleash your inner power and resilience in every aspect of your life.

Case Study: Kristin

Kristin, a 35-year-old marketing executive, had always prided herself on her ability to handle high-pressure situations at work. However, when she was passed over for a promotion she had been working toward for years, she found herself struggling to cope with the overwhelming emotions that followed.

Feeling a mix of anger, disappointment, and self-doubt, Kristin initially tried to suppress her emotions and push through her daily responsibilities. She told herself that she needed to be mentally tough and that these feelings were a sign of weakness. However, as the weeks passed, she found herself becoming more irritable, less focused, and increasingly disengaged from her work and personal life.

Recognizing that her current approach wasn't serving her, Kristin decided to seek guidance from a coach specializing in emotional intelligence and resilience. Through her work with the coach, Kristin began to understand the importance of emotional agility in maintaining mental toughness.

She learned to

- acknowledge and accept her emotions without judgment, recognizing that they were valid responses to a challenging situation.
- practice mindfulness to observe her thoughts and feelings without getting caught up in them, creating space for clarity and intentional action.
- challenge her assumptions and reframe her perspective, looking for opportunities for growth and learning in the face of adversity.
- cultivate self-compassion, treating herself with kindness and understanding rather than harsh self-criticism.
- develop a proactive resilience plan, identifying her strengths, support systems, and coping strategies to navigate future challenges.

As Kristin began to incorporate these emotional agility practices into her daily life, she noticed a significant shift in her mindset and well-being. Rather than feeling overwhelmed and controlled by her emotions, she developed the flexibility and resilience to navigate her inner world with greater ease and intention.

With her newfound emotional agility, Kristin was able to approach her work with renewed focus and motivation. She started to view the missed promotion as an opportunity to reassess her career goals and develop new skills. She also became a more supportive and understanding leader for her team, creating a culture of openness and resilience in the face of challenges.

Kristin's journey to emotional agility not only transformed her ability to cope with the disappointment of the missed promotion but also equipped her with the inner strength and flexibility to thrive in the face of future adversities. By embracing her emotions as valuable sources of insight and learning, Kristin discovered that true mental toughness lay in her ability to adapt, grow, and move forward with intention and grace.

Encourage Others to Listen to Their Emotions

 The human capacity for burden is like bamboo — far more flexible than you'd ever believe at first glance.

Jodi Picoult

Earlier in this book, I shared the story of Kate — a woman who had lost her job and thought her world would fall apart, only to discover her immense resilience. The first step toward her progress lay in recognizing the full gamut of her emotions, including sadness about having invested so much in an employer who no longer had a place for her, and worry about her future financial stability.

Vulnerability is a buzzword on the current mental health and wellness scene, but it's just the tip of the iceberg. Embracing your imperfection, asking for support, and taking risks are all key components of resilience, but so, too, is listening to your emotions.

Anger, fear, sadness, disappointment… these are all powerful signs that it's time to make much-needed changes. Within the discomfort and pain they bring lie the kernels of change. Resilience isn't about putting on a brave face and hiding what we feel. Quite the opposite. It's about feeling emotion, understanding that challenges are what make us grow, and pushing through the pain.

I hope that by this stage in your reading, you have seen how big life changes and obstacles can lead you to positive choices such as embracing mindfulness, managing stress proactively, and honing your mental agility. If the strategies in this book have made a difference in your life, then you're in the perfect position to help someone else.

By leaving a review on Amazon, you'll help other readers discover the key steps they need to take to move beyond life's biggest setbacks.

Share your opinion of this book and a little bit about your own story. One of the most powerful ways to boost your own strength is to help others hone theirs.

Thank you for your support. Together, we can shine the light on the transformative power of our thoughts and emotions.

Scan the QR code

FIVE

Step #4—Skyrocket Your Confidence

 You never know how strong you are, until being strong is your only choice.

Bob Marley

Self-doubt. Imposter syndrome. Negative self-talk. We've all experienced those confidence-draining thoughts that make us question our abilities and self-worth. But here's the truth: Confidence isn't just a feel-good emotion—it's a crucial ingredient in the recipe for mental toughness. When you believe in yourself and your capabilities, you're far more likely to persevere in the face of challenges and bounce back from setbacks.

In this chapter, we'll unpack what genuine confidence looks like, why it's so vital for a resilient mindset, and practical strategies you can start implementing today to boost your self-assurance. Get ready to begin seeing yourself in a whole new light!

The Value of Confidence

So, what exactly do we mean by confidence? In essence, confidence is a feeling of trust in your qualities, abilities, and judgment. It's an inner knowing that you're capable of handling what life throws at you. Confident people exude a sense of calm self-assurance and are willing to take risks, seize opportunities, and stand up for what they believe in.

But make no mistake—confidence isn't about being immune to fear or never experiencing self-doubt. Even the most self-assured among us have moments when we second-guess ourselves. The difference lies in not allowing those doubts to paralyze or hold you back from going after what you want.

Why is confidence so crucial for mental toughness? For starters, confidence empowers you to step outside your comfort zone. When you have faith in your abilities, you're more likely to take on new challenges, pursue ambitious goals, and embrace the discomfort that comes with growth and learning.

Additionally, confidence helps you maintain perspective and reframe obstacles as opportunities. Rather than being derailed by setbacks, a confident mindset enables you to extract valuable lessons from failures and keep moving forward. You're also better equipped to advocate for yourself, set healthy boundaries, and make self-honoring choices.

Common Barriers to Confidence

If self-confidence is so important, why do so many of us struggle with it? The reality is that there are numerous barriers that can chip away at even the heartiest of self-esteem. Some common confidence killers include:

- **Perfectionism and fear of failure.** When you equate your worth with flawless performance, the pressure to "get it right" can be paralyzing.
- **Comparison and competition.** In our social-media saturated world, it's easy to fall into the trap of measuring yourself against curated highlight reels and feeling like you're falling short.
- **Lack of self-compassion.** Confident people aren't immune to inner critics, but they know how to respond to themselves with kindness and understanding rather than harsh judgment.
- **Scarcity mindset.** If you're prone to "never enough" thinking, you may have trouble internalizing your accomplishments and valuing what you bring to the table.

If any of these barriers resonate with you, take heart in knowing that confidence is not a fixed trait but a skill that can be cultivated and strengthened.

Solution #1: Celebrate the Small Things

One of the simplest yet most impactful ways to skyrocket your confidence is to start acknowledging your wins, however small they may seem. By celebrating minor milestones and accomplishments, you gradually build a reservoir of positive evidence that boosts your self-assurance.

Why Celebrating Small Victories Matters

When you get in the habit of recognizing your daily efforts and achievements, you train your brain to focus on success rather than dwelling on shortcomings. This shift in perspective is crucial for cultivating a resilient, confident mindset.

Celebrating small wins also helps counteract the negative bias that often plagues our self-perception. Our brains are wired to pay more attention to failures and mistakes than to successes and triumphs. By intentionally highlighting your victories, you create a more balanced and accurate view of your abilities.

Moreover, acknowledging minor milestones provides a steady stream of motivation and encouragement. When you take the time to savor your progress, you're more likely to stay engaged and persistent in the face of challenges. Each small win becomes a building block of confidence, propelling you forward.

How to Make It a Habit

To start harnessing the power of small victories, try implementing these simple practices:

- **Keep a daily success log:** At the end of each day, write down three things you accomplished or handled well. These don't have to be monumental feats—simply cooking a nourishing meal or tackling a dreaded email counts.
- **Share your wins with others:** Don't be afraid to celebrate your successes with supportive friends, family, or colleagues. Their recognition and encouragement can further bolster your confidence.
- **Savor the moment:** When you achieve a goal or milestone, take a few minutes to fully appreciate the experience. Notice how it feels in your body and mind to have succeeded.
- **Reframe challenges as opportunities:** When faced with a difficult task or situation, ask yourself, "How can I break this down into manageable steps and create small wins along the way?"

By consistently celebrating your small victories, you'll develop a more confident, resilient mindset. You'll start to notice and appreciate your strengths, skills, and accomplishments, creating a positive feedback loop that fuels further success.

Solution #2: Hone a Growth Mindset

The way you think about skills and abilities has a huge impact on your confidence levels. Cultivating a growth mindset—the belief that you can improve and expand your abilities through effort and learning—is a game-changer for building self-assurance.

Fixed vs. Growth: Two Ways of Thinking

While the concepts of fixed and growth mindsets are discussed briefly in *Mastering Emotional Intelligence With Ease*, they also have significant relevance to developing mental toughness. According to research by psychologist Carol Dweck, people generally fall into two camps when it comes to their beliefs about ability: those with a fixed mindset and those with a growth mindset (2012).

If you have a fixed mindset, you tend to view talents and intelligence as static, unchangeable traits. You believe that you're either naturally good at something or you're not. With this perspective, challenges and setbacks become threats to your sense of competence and worth.

In contrast, a growth mindset sees skills and abilities as malleable qualities that can be developed over time. If you have a growth orientation, you view challenges as opportunities to learn and improve. Mistakes and failures aren't indicative of a lack of talent but rather stepping stones to mastery.

Benefits of a Growth Mindset

Adopting a growth mindset is a powerful way to enhance your confidence and resilience. When you trust in your capacity to learn and grow, you're less likely to be derailed by self-doubt or fear of failure.

A growth mindset also fosters a healthier relationship with risk-taking and setbacks. Instead of shying away from challenges or beating yourself up over mistakes, you embrace difficulty as a chance to stretch beyond your comfort zone. You view failure as feedback to learn from rather than a judgment of your worth.

Furthermore, a growth mindset allows you to find inspiration in the success of others rather than feeling threatened or discouraged by their accomplishments. You recognize that their triumphs are proof of what's possible through dedication and effort.

Cultivating a Growth-Oriented Mindset

To start shifting from a fixed to a growth mindset, try implementing these practices:

- **Embrace the power of "yet":** When you catch yourself thinking, *I'm not good at this*, add the word "yet" to the end of the sentence. Remind yourself that your current abilities aren't fixed or final.
- **Reframe challenges as learning opportunities:** When faced with a difficult task or situation, ask yourself, "What can I learn from this?" instead of "What if I fail?"
- **Celebrate effort and progress, not just results:** Recognize the hard work and strategies that go into your successes, not just the end outcome. Focus on the process of growth rather than fixating on perfection.

- **Learn from the successes of others:** When you witness someone else thriving, get curious about their journey. What mindsets and practices have they cultivated to reach that point? Use their example as inspiration and proof of what's possible.

By consciously shifting toward a growth mindset, you'll develop unshakable confidence in your ability to learn, improve, and achieve your goals. Setbacks and challenges will become stepping stones to success rather than threats to your sense of self. You'll approach life with a newfound sense of curiosity, resilience, and self-assurance.

Solution #3: Engage

One of the most powerful ways to supercharge your confidence is to take a proactive stance in your life. Confidence is ultimately a result of doing, learning, and growing—not just thinking or preparing. By embracing challenges and new experiences, you'll cultivate an unshakable trust in your abilities.

Engagement: The Key to Confidence

It's easy to fall into the trap of "analysis paralysis"—endlessly researching, planning, and ruminating rather than actually diving in. But true confidence emerges from putting yourself out there and engaging with life wholeheartedly.

When you take bold action, even in the face of fear or uncertainty, you send a powerful message to your subconscious mind. You affirm your belief in your ability to handle challenges and navigate new terrain. Each courageous step reinforces the notion that you are capable, competent, and resilient.

Moreover, taking action allows you to gather real-world evidence of your abilities. As you tackle new challenges and learn from your experiences, you'll develop a robust sense of self-efficacy—the belief in your capacity to succeed. This self-trust is the foundation of unshakeable confidence.

Strategies for Bold Engagement

To start building your confidence through courageous action, try these strategies:

- **Pursue flow-inducing hobbies:** Engage in activities that fully absorb your attention and allow you to lose yourself in the process. These "flow states" provide a powerful boost of confidence and self-assurance.
- **Set stretch goals:** Challenge yourself to step outside your comfort zone regularly. Set ambitious goals that require you to grow and expand your skills. Remember, the aim isn't perfection but rather consistent progress.
- **Embrace discomfort:** Recognize that feeling uncomfortable is often a sign that you're growing and learning. Lean into that discomfort and view it as a positive signal that you're becoming more confident and capable.
- **Learn voraciously:** Continuously seek out opportunities to gain knowledge and sharpen your abilities. Read books, attend workshops, seek mentorship—immerse yourself in the process of self-improvement.
- **Fail forward:** Reframe failures and setbacks as valuable learning experiences. Instead of letting them shake your confidence, view them as stepping stones to mastery. Cultivate the resilience to bounce back and keep moving forward.

By consistently taking bold, courageous action, you'll cultivate a strong sense of confidence and self-assurance. You'll develop a deep trust in your ability to handle whatever challenges come your way, knowing that each experience is an opportunity to learn, grow, and become the best version of yourself.

Wrapping Up...

In this chapter, we delved into the transformative power of confidence in cultivating mental toughness. By recognizing the immense value of self-assurance and implementing practical strategies to boost your confidence, you lay the foundation for unshakable resilience in the face of any challenge.

We've explored a range of essential techniques to boost your confidence, including:

- embracing a growth mindset to view challenges as opportunities for learning and improvement
- celebrating small victories to build a reservoir of positive evidence and boost self-assurance
- engaging in flow-inducing hobbies and setting stretch goals to build confidence through courageous action

Confidence is the fuel that propels you forward, empowering you to take bold action, seize opportunities, and bounce back from setbacks with renewed determination. By cultivating an unshakable belief in your abilities and potential, you'll be equipped to tackle even the most daunting challenges head-on.

As we continue our exploration of mental toughness, the next chapter will invite us to take control of one of our most precious resources: time. We'll dive into game-changing strategies for mastering productivity, prioritizing your goals, and designing a life that truly lights you up. Get ready to shift from a reactive to a proactive mindset as you learn to make every moment count and achieve your wildest dreams with unwavering focus and efficiency.

Case Study: Robert

Robert, a 48-year-old high school teacher, had always been passionate about education and making a difference in his students' lives. However, despite his years of experience and dedication to his craft, Robert often found himself plagued by self-doubt and a nagging sense that he wasn't truly making an impact.

As he watched younger, more tech-savvy teachers join the faculty and effortlessly connect with students, Robert began to question his own abilities and relevance. He shied away from taking on new initiatives or speaking up in faculty meetings, fearing that his ideas were outdated or unworthy of consideration.

Recognizing that his lack of confidence was not only impacting his professional growth but also his ability to be the best possible educator for his students, Robert resolved to take action. He started by exploring the root causes of his self-doubt, tracing it back to a deeply ingrained belief that he was "too old to learn new tricks" and a tendency to compare himself unfavorably to his colleagues.

Armed with this self-awareness, Robert embarked on a journey to rebuild his confidence from the inside out. He began by celebrating the small victories in his classroom each day, whether it was a student's "aha" moment during a lesson or a heartfelt thank-you from a graduating senior. These moments served as powerful reminders of his impact and value as an educator.

Robert also made a conscious effort to adopt a growth mindset, viewing challenges and setbacks as opportunities for learning and development. He enrolled in professional development workshops to expand his skill set, particularly in areas like technology integration and student-centered learning. As he stepped outside his comfort zone and acquired new knowledge, Robert began to see himself as a lifelong learner rather than someone whose best days were behind him.

To further boost his confidence, Robert sought out a mentor in the form of a veteran teacher who had successfully navigated the evolving landscape of education. This mentor provided guidance, support, and encouragement as Robert took on new challenges and explored innovative teaching strategies.

Alongside these efforts, Robert reconnected with his love for hiking and nature photography, hobbies that had fallen by the wayside in the busyness of life. He carved out time each weekend to hit the trails, finding solace and renewal in the great outdoors. As he immersed himself in these confidence-fueling pursuits, Robert found his sense of self-assurance and resilience spilled over into his teaching.

Gradually, Robert began to notice a profound shift in his mindset and presence in the classroom. He approached his lessons with newfound enthusiasm and creativity, unafraid to take risks and try new approaches. His students responded to his renewed energy and confidence, leading to deeper engagement and more meaningful learning experiences.

Perhaps most significantly, Robert learned to silence his inner critic and embrace his unique strengths as an educator. He came to understand that his experience, wisdom, and dedication were invaluable assets and that he had the power to continue making a profound difference in his students' lives.

Through his journey, Robert discovered that confidence is not about being perfect or having all the answers but rather about trusting in one's ability to learn, grow, and make a meaningful impact. By combining practical strategies like celebrating small wins, embracing a growth mindset, seeking out mentorship, and engaging in fulfilling hobbies, he was able to rewrite his internal narrative and tap into his full potential as an educator.

Robert's story serves as a powerful reminder that it's never too late to invest in oneself and cultivate unshakable confidence. His journey highlights that true mental toughness is not about the absence of fear or doubt but rather the resilience and self-belief to keep moving forward in the pursuit of one's passions and purpose.

SIX

Step #5—Time is Ticking... Better Manage It!

We don't even know how strong we are until we are forced to bring that hidden strength forward.

Isabel Allende

Do you constantly feel like there aren't enough hours in the day? Like no matter how hard you try, you just can't seem to get a handle on your time and responsibilities? If so, you're far from alone. In today's fast-paced world, poor time management is one of the most common barriers to achieving mental toughness and resilience.

When we allow time to slip through our fingers, it leads to missed deadlines, forgotten commitments, and a perpetual state of feeling overwhelmed. This chronic stress erodes our confidence and inner strength. Pretty soon, we feel totally out of control, helplessly adrift in a chaotic sea of obligations and unfinished business.

But here's the good news—it doesn't have to be this way. With the right time management strategies, you can take back the reins, reduce your stress levels, and build the mental fortitude to handle whatever life throws your way. In this chapter, I'll share some of the most effective techniques for mastering your minutes and harnessing your hours. Get ready to feel empowered, productive, and mentally tough!

The Time Management Tango

What exactly do we mean by "time management" anyway? At its core, time management is the process of organizing and planning how to allocate your hours to specific activities. It's about working smarter, not harder, to achieve maximum productivity and minimum stress, especially when deadlines are tight and pressures are high.

Time management is a skill that involves goal setting, planning, prioritizing, and controlling how much time you spend on specific tasks. It's about using your time wisely and efficiently to achieve your goals and reach your full potential. Good time management allows you to work smarter, not harder, so you can get more done in less time, even when pressures are high.

Signs of effective time management include:

- prioritizing important tasks
- meeting deadlines consistently
- feeling in control of your schedule
- having time for strategic planning
- maintaining work–life balance
- staying focused with minimal distractions
- delegating when appropriate
- communicating timelines clearly

In contrast, poor time managers tend to:

- miss deadlines frequently
- procrastinate on important projects
- feel perpetually stressed and overwhelmed
- neglect planning and work reactively instead
- struggle with work–life boundaries
- get sidetracked by low-priority interruptions
- hoard tasks rather than delegating
- overpromise and underdeliver

Effective time management is crucial for achieving goals, reducing stress, and improving overall quality of life. When you have good time management skills, you feel more in control of your day, leading to lower stress levels and improved mental well-being. This enables you to be more productive and efficient, produce higher quality work, make better decisions, and have more free time for hobbies and relationships. As a result, you feel more accomplished and satisfied, experience less burnout and fatigue, and can adapt to changes and unexpected events more easily. Ultimately, effective time management helps you achieve long-term goals and career advancement.

Conversely, poor time management can lead to missed deadlines, subpar work quality, strained relationships, chronic stress, and diminished mental toughness. When you're constantly behind the eight ball, it's hard to muster the resilience to bounce back from setbacks.

As you can see, stellar time management offers incredible benefits for your well-being and performance. When you're in the driver's seat of your day, you feel calmer, more competent, and more resilient overall. You're able to be proactive rather than reactive, which is a hallmark of mental toughness.

In short, mastering time management is a major key to unlocking your inner strength and weathering life's storms. So, let's dive into some practical solutions you can implement to hone your skills.

Solution #1: Prioritization

Not all tasks are created equal. To manage your time effectively, you need to get crystal clear on your highest priorities and tackle those first. When everything feels urgent, prioritization provides a roadmap through the overwhelm. By taking decisive action on your most important activities, you build momentum, motivation, and mental muscle.

Prioritizing tasks means evaluating their importance and urgency and then ranking them in order of priority. When you prioritize effectively, you focus your time and energy on the most critical and valuable tasks, rather than getting bogged down in busywork or distractions.

Prioritizing offers numerous benefits, including improved focus and concentration, greater efficiency and productivity, enhanced decision-making abilities, reduced stress and anxiety, and an increased sense of control and accomplishment. By prioritizing, you create more time for important goals and relationships while developing the ability to adapt to changing circumstances.

There are several frameworks you can use to determine your priorities:

- **The Eisenhower Matrix:** This classic tool helps you sort tasks into four boxes based on urgency and importance:

  - Urgent and Important: Do these tasks immediately
  - Not Urgent but Important: Schedule these tasks

○ Urgent but Not Important: Delegate these tasks
○ Not Urgent and Not Important: Delete these tasks

- **RICE:** This acronym stands for Reach, Impact, Confidence, and Effort. Score tasks on a scale of 1–10 in each of these areas. Tasks with the highest total score become your top priorities.

- **ABCDE Method:** Start by making a master list of everything on your plate. Then, assign each task a letter:

  ○ A: Tasks you must do—serious consequences if not completed
  ○ B: Tasks you should do—mild consequences if not completed
  ○ C: Tasks that would be nice to do but have no consequences if not completed
  ○ D: Tasks that can be delegated to someone else
  ○ E: Tasks that can be eliminated entirely

The key to making any of these methods work is consistency. Make prioritization a daily habit, ideally at the start of each day or the night before. Ask yourself: What are the most important things I need to accomplish today? This week? This month? Then, align your time and attention accordingly.

It can also be helpful to use visual cues, like highlighting or starring top priorities in your planner or task list. The more front-of-mind your high-impact activities are, the less likely you are to get sidetracked by shiny distractions.

Remember, saying yes to one thing means saying no to something else. Be judicious about what you allow onto your plate, and be willing to let go of tasks that don't align with your highest goals and values. Mentally tough people know that focus and follow-through beat running around like a chicken with your head cut off any day.

Solution #2: Planning and Strategies

Once you're clear on your priorities, it's time to translate them into a well-crafted plan. Mentally tough people understand the necessity of preparation and strategy. As the old adage goes, "failing to plan is planning to fail."

Planning is the process of charting out the specific actions needed to achieve a goal. It involves breaking down a large project into smaller, manageable steps, setting deadlines, and identifying any resources or support you'll need along the way.

Effective planning offers several key benefits:

- provides clarity and direction
- improves efficiency and productivity
- reduces stress and anxiety
- increases chances of success
- allows for better resource allocation
- facilitates communication and collaboration
- enables course correction when needed

Here are some of the most effective time management planning strategies to build into your routine:

Time blocking: This technique involves dividing your day into distinct blocks of time, each dedicated to a specific activity. For example, you might block off 9–10 a.m. for strategic planning, 10 a.m.–12 p.m. for focused work on a high-priority project, 12 p.m.–1 p.m. for lunch and movement, 1–2 p.m. for meetings, and so on.

Time blocking combats our tendency to work reactively and get thrown off course by interruptions. It creates hard edges in your schedule, ensuring meaningful progress on your most important tasks. To make it work:

- Identify your high-priority tasks and estimate how long they'll take.
- Group similar activities together (e.g., all your calls or errands).
- Build in buffer time for the unexpected.
- Communicate your availability to others.
- Honor your blocks as non-negotiable appointments.

Using a planner: Don't try to juggle everything in your head. Invest in a physical or digital planning tool where you can capture tasks, appointments, deadlines, and ideas. Putting pen to paper clears mental clutter and helps you feel grounded.

When selecting a planner, consider:

- format (daily, weekly, monthly)
- size and portability
- customization options
- goal-setting and review pages
- bonus features like habit trackers or gratitude prompts

Each night, take a few minutes to review the day ahead. Ask yourself: What are my top three priorities? What might trip me up, and how can I stay on track? A little bit of intention goes a long way.

To-do lists: In addition to time blocking, maintain a running log of tasks on deck. But rather than throwing everything on one giant list, separate tasks into a few key categories:

- Master list: Capture everything swirling in your head in one place.
- Daily list: Pull a handful of items from your Master List to tackle today.
- Priority list: Note your top 1–3 most critical/valuable tasks.

You can also segment lists by project, timeframe (e.g., this week vs. next), or type (e.g., calls to make, errands to run). The key is to have a go-to reference for staying organized and focused.

To make your lists work for you:

- Keep them short and realistic—aim for 3–5 items per day.
- Use actionable language (e.g., "Draft proposal" vs. "Work on proposal").
- Assign due dates and estimate the time needed.
- Cross off completed items for a sense of progress.
- Review and update regularly.

Again, prioritization is paramount. Always highlight your top three to-dos and weigh those most heavily. Don't fall into the trap of confusing being busy with being productive.

Planning and preparation are key ingredients in the recipe for mental toughness. When you take the time to chart your course, anticipate obstacles, and build in contingencies, you feel more capable and in control. You're able to weather life's curveballs with greater equanimity because you have a clear sense of direction and purpose.

Solution #3: Letting Go of the Extra

Even the best-laid plans can go awry if you're drowning in excess. Mentally tough people know that addition by subtraction is a real thing. Lightening your load is a prerequisite to following through on what matters most.

Overcommitting is a common trap that can sabotage even the most well-intentioned time management efforts. When you try to do too much, you end up doing nothing well. You're spread thin, stressed out, and unable to give your full focus and energy to your highest priorities.

Learning to let go of extraneous responsibilities and obligations is a critical skill for boosting mental strength and resilience. It allows you to reclaim your time, attention, and energy for the things that truly matter to you.

Here's how to start identifying what commitments or obligations you may need to release:

1. Write down everything currently on your plate (work projects, side hustles, volunteer roles, committees, social clubs, etc.).
2. Give each a score from 1–10 based on (a) how much you enjoy it and (b) how much it contributes to your highest goals/values.
3. Highlight any items with a combined score of less than 10.
4. Ask yourself: What would happen if I didn't do this anymore? What's the worst case scenario? The best case?
5. Notice any fears or limiting beliefs that arise (e.g., "I don't want to let anyone down" or "I'm not allowed to say no").
6. Start with the lowest-scored item and take one small step to release or reduce that commitment.

This process can be challenging, especially if you're used to being the go-to person or pride yourself on having a full plate. But remember, every time you say "yes" to something, you're saying "no" to something else—including your precious time and energy.

Some strategies that can help ease the transition:

- Look for opportunities to delegate, automate, or simplify before eliminating altogether.
- Communicate proactively about changes to set expectations and avoid dropping the ball.
- Offer alternative resources or solutions when you do say no.
- Practice self-compassion—releasing something doesn't make you a failure or flake.
- Focus forward on what you're saying YES to (more whitespace, more buckets filled).

Mentally strong people understand that doing less can often mean accomplishing more. They're willing to make tough choices about where to invest their resources, even if it means disappointing others in the short term. They know that creating space for what matters most is the path to fulfillment and inner peace.

Wrapping Up...

We've covered a lot of ground in this chapter. To recap, time management is a critical skill for cultivating mental toughness and resilience. When you're at the mercy of your calendar, everything feels harder. But when you take charge of your days with intentionality and strategy, you tap into deep wells of inner power and poise.

The three keys to stellar time management are:

- **Prioritization:** Getting crystal clear on what matters most and tackling those items first
- **Planning:** Implementing proven strategies like time blocking and list-making to stay organized and on track
- **Pruning:** Letting go of extraneous commitments to free up bandwidth for your highest-impact activities

With these tools in hand, you're well on your way to feeling grounded, empowered, and in control no matter what life brings your way. You'll be able to meet challenges with greater confidence and equanimity, knowing that you're focused on what truly matters.

But time management is just one piece of the mental toughness puzzle. In the next chapter, we'll dive into another critical component: the art of setting and upholding healthy boundaries. Get ready to communicate your needs with clarity and conviction so you can stay true to yourself in the face of life's demands.

Case Study: Erika

Erika was a busy marketing manager who constantly felt overwhelmed and stressed out. Despite working long hours and weekends, she always seemed to be behind on her deadlines and commitments. Her work quality was suffering, and she had little time or energy left for her personal life and relationships.

One day, Erika reached a breaking point. She knew something had to change if she wanted to regain control of her life and build the mental resilience to handle her demanding career. She decided to seek out a time management coach to help her develop new skills and strategies.

The first thing Erika's coach had her do was a time audit. For one week, Erika tracked how she spent every minute of her day, from the moment she woke up until she went to bed. The results were eye-opening. Erika realized she was wasting hours each day on low-priority tasks, distractions, and interruptions. She was constantly reacting to other people's demands rather than proactively focusing on her own goals and priorities.

Armed with this insight, Erika and her coach set about creating a new time management plan. They started by clarifying Erika's top priorities and values, both at work and in her personal life. Erika realized that she had been neglecting her health, relationships, and creative passions in favor of work demands that often weren't even that important.

Next, Erika learned how to use the Eisenhower Matrix to categorize her tasks based on urgency and importance. She committed to spending the majority of her time on important but not urgent activities like strategic planning, skill development, and relationship building. She also set boundaries around her availability, communicating to her team when she would be working on focused solo tasks and when she was available for meetings and collaboration.

Erika also implemented time blocking to create dedicated chunks of time for different types of activities. She blocked off her mornings for deep work on her highest priority projects, her afternoons for meetings and administrative tasks, and her evenings for exercise, family time, and hobbies. She used a digital calendar to schedule these blocks and communicated her plan to her team and family.

To stay organized and on track, Erika started using a bullet journal to capture and prioritize her daily and weekly tasks. She also conducted a weekly review to celebrate her accomplishments, identify areas for improvement, and plan for the week ahead.

Finally, Erika took a hard look at her commitments and started practicing the art of saying no. She realized she had been over-committing out of a sense of guilt and a desire to please others. But by being more selective about what she took on, she was able to create more space for the things that truly mattered to her.

As Erika implemented these new strategies, she started to see significant improvements in her productivity, stress levels, and overall well-being. She was able to meet her deadlines with less rushing and cramming, and she had more time and energy for her personal life. She felt more in control and mentally strong, even when faced with challenging projects or tight turnarounds.

Perhaps most importantly, Erika's newfound time mastery allowed her to be more strategic and proactive in her career. Instead of just reacting to the demands of her job, she was able to carve out time for big-picture thinking, professional development, and building strong relationships with her team and stakeholders. She even started a passion project on the side, something she never would have had the bandwidth for before.

Through her journey, Erika learned that time management isn't just about being more efficient or productive. It's about aligning your time and energy with your deepest values and priorities. It's about creating a life that feels meaningful, fulfilling, and mentally strong. And while it takes effort and discipline, the payoff is more than worth it.

SEVEN

Step #6—Forming Boundaries (and Helping Them Stick)

 The greatest glory in living lies not in never falling, but in rising every time we fall.

Nelson Mandela

I magine a life without boundaries—a life where you say yes to every request, take on more than you can handle, and let others dictate your time and energy. Sounds exhausting, doesn't it? That's because it is. Living without clear boundaries is a surefire recipe for stress, resentment, and burnout. It's like having a beautiful garden with no fence to protect it from trampling feet and hungry critters. Pretty soon, your inner landscape is a mess of overturned soil and wilted blooms.

But here's the good news: Setting and maintaining healthy boundaries is a skill that anyone can learn. And it's a skill that's absolutely essential for cultivating mental toughness and resilience. When you know your limits and communicate them clearly, you create the space and safety you need to thrive. You're able to focus your energy on what matters most without getting sidetracked by other people's agendas or expectations.

In this chapter, we'll explore the power of boundaries in depth. You'll learn what boundaries are, why they're so important, and how to identify and set your own. We'll also cover strategies for communicating your boundaries with kindness and clarity, even in the face of pushback or resistance. By the end, you'll have a toolbox full of techniques for creating and sustaining the boundaries you need to be your best self. Let's dive in!

Everyone Needs Boundaries

So what exactly are boundaries, anyway? Put simply, boundaries are the limits we set to protect our time, energy, and well-being. They're the invisible lines that define what we will and won't accept in our relationships and interactions with others.

Think of boundaries like the walls of a castle. They provide structure, security, and a clear delineation between what's inside (your priorities, values, and needs) and what's outside (other people's demands and expectations). Just like a castle needs strong walls to withstand siege and invasion, you need solid boundaries to maintain your mental and emotional fortitude.

Some common examples of personal boundaries include:

- saying no to requests that don't align with your goals or values
- asking others not to comment on your appearance or weight
- limiting the amount of time you spend on social media or responding to emails outside of work hours

- declining invitations to events or activities that don't interest you or fit your schedule
- requesting that people respect your privacy and personal space
- communicating your needs and expectations clearly in relationships
- taking time for self-care and solitude without feeling guilty

At their core, boundaries are about honoring your own needs and desires. They're a way of saying "this is what works for me" and "this is what doesn't." By setting clear boundaries, you teach others how to treat you and show up for yourself with authenticity and integrity.

Boundaries are also crucial for maintaining healthy relationships. When everyone knows where they stand and what's expected of them, there's less room for misunderstanding, resentment, and conflict. Boundaries create a sense of safety and trust that allows intimacy and connection to flourish.

But perhaps most importantly, boundaries are essential for cultivating mental toughness and resilience. When you have strong boundaries in place, you're less likely to take on other people's stress or get caught up in drama that's not yours to solve. You're able to stay focused on your own goals and priorities, even in the face of outside pressure or distractions.

Boundaries also help you build self-respect and confidence. When you honor your own limits and needs, you send a powerful message to yourself and others that you matter. You reinforce the belief that your time, energy, and well-being are valuable and deserving of protection.

Without clear boundaries, it's all too easy to get swept up in other people's agendas and lose sight of your own. You may find yourself saying yes when you really want to say no, taking on more than you can handle, or sacrificing your own needs for the sake of others. Over time, this can lead to feelings of resentment, exhaustion, and even burnout.

But with strong boundaries in place, you create a buffer against the chaos and demands of the world. You're able to stay grounded in your own truth and make choices that align with your deepest values and desires. You're able to weather life's storms with greater ease and resilience because you know where you stand and what you stand for.

Of course, setting and maintaining boundaries is often easier said than done. Many of us have been conditioned from a young age to be accommodating, self-sacrificing, and "nice." We may worry that setting boundaries will make us seem selfish or uncaring or that we'll face backlash or rejection if we say no.

But the truth is, setting boundaries is one of the most caring things you can do—for yourself and for others. When you're clear about your limits and needs, you create the conditions for genuine, mutually satisfying relationships. You teach others how to respect and value you, and you model healthy self-care and self-advocacy.

So how do you go about setting and maintaining boundaries in a way that feels authentic and empowering? Let's explore some practical strategies.

Solution #1: Understand Your Boundaries

The first step in setting effective boundaries is getting clear on what your boundaries actually are. This may seem obvious, but many of us have never taken the time to really think about what we need and want in our relationships and interactions.

One way to start identifying your boundaries is to pay attention to your gut reactions. Notice when you feel resentful, anxious, or overwhelmed in response to someone else's words or actions. These uncomfortable emotions are often a sign that a boundary has been crossed or needs to be set.

For example, let's say you have a coworker who consistently interrupts you during meetings or takes credit for your ideas. You may feel irritated, disrespected, or even angry in these moments. That's a clue that you need to set a boundary around communication and collaboration.

Or perhaps you have a friend who frequently cancels plans at the last minute or shows up late without apology. You may feel hurt, disappointed, or taken for granted. That's a sign that you need to set a boundary around reliability and respect for your time.

Another way to identify your boundaries is to reflect on your values and priorities. What's most important to you in your relationships and interactions? What do you need to feel safe, respected, and valued? What are your non-negotiables?

For instance, honesty and transparency may be top values for you. That means you need relationships where there's open communication and no hidden agendas. Or perhaps work–life balance is a key priority. That means you need to set boundaries around your availability outside of work hours and protect your personal time.

Some other common boundaries include:

- Physical boundaries: your personal space, privacy, and physical touch

- Emotional boundaries: your feelings, thoughts, and ability to separate your emotions from others'
- Time boundaries: how you spend your time, how much time you give to others, and how much alone time you need
- Material boundaries: your money, possessions, and resources
- Intellectual boundaries: your ideas, creativity, and credit for your work
- Sexual boundaries: your comfort level with sexual touch, activity, and communication

Everyone's boundaries will be different based on their unique needs, values, and experiences. What's important is that you take the time to reflect on what matters most to you and what you need to feel safe and supported.

Once you have a sense of your key boundaries, it can be helpful to write them down and refer back to them often. You might make a list of your "non-negotiables" or create a personal bill of rights. The more clarity and conviction you have around your boundaries, the easier it will be to communicate and uphold them.

Solution #2: Setting Boundaries

Once you know what your boundaries are, the next step is actually setting them. This means communicating your limits and needs clearly and directly to others.

Setting boundaries can feel scary at first, especially if you're not used to standing up for yourself. You may worry about coming across as rude or aggressive, or fear that others will reject or abandon you if you say no.

But remember, setting boundaries is not about controlling others or making them change. It's about taking responsibility for your own well-being and communicating what you need to thrive. When you set boundaries from a place of clarity and compassion, others are more likely to respond positively and respectfully.

Here are some tips for setting effective boundaries:

- **Be direct and specific.** Avoid hinting, hedging, or apologizing for your needs. Use clear, concise language to state your boundary firmly and kindly. For example, instead of saying, "I'm sorry, I'm just so busy lately," try, "I appreciate the invitation, but I'm not available to take on any new commitments right now."
- **Use "I" statements.** Focus on expressing your own needs and feelings rather than blaming or attacking others. For instance, instead of saying, "You always take advantage of me," try, "I feel overwhelmed when I'm asked to take on last-minute requests. I need more advance notice to plan my time effectively."
- **Be consistent.** Boundaries only work if you enforce them consistently. If you set a boundary and then let it slide, others will learn that your limits are negotiable. It's important to follow through and hold firm, even if it feels uncomfortable at first.
- **Start small.** If you're new to setting boundaries, it's okay to start with small, low-stakes requests and work your way up. For example, you might practice saying no to a minor request from a coworker before tackling a more challenging conversation with a family member.
- **Expect some pushback.** Not everyone will be thrilled about your new boundaries, and that's okay. Some people may try to guilt trip you, argue with you, or ignore your

requests altogether. Remember, their reaction is not your responsibility. Stay focused on what you need and trust that the right people will respect your limits.

- **Seek support.** Setting and maintaining boundaries can be tough, especially if you have a history of people-pleasing or codependency. Don't be afraid to seek support from a therapist, coach, or trusted friend as you navigate this new terrain. Having a cheerleader in your corner can make all the difference.

It's also important to remember that boundaries are not a one-time conversation. They require ongoing communication and reinforcement. As your needs and circumstances change, your boundaries may need to evolve as well. Be willing to reassess and adjust as needed, and keep the lines of communication open with the people in your life.

Solution #3: (Re)enforcing Boundaries

Even with the best of intentions and the clearest of communication, there will be times when others cross your boundaries. Maybe a friend keeps showing up unannounced, or a coworker continues to send you non-urgent emails on the weekends. When this happens, it's important to have strategies in place for reinforcing your limits and protecting your well-being.

The first step is to recognize when a boundary has been violated. Pay attention to your emotions and physical sensations. Do you feel resentful, anxious, or drained? Is your jaw clenched or your stomach in knots? These are all signs that someone may have overstepped your limits.

Once you've identified that a boundary has been crossed, it's important to address it as soon as possible. The longer you wait, the harder it will be to speak up and the more likely you are to harbor resentment or let the behavior continue unchecked.

When communicating about a boundary violation, use the same clear, direct language you used when setting the boundary in the first place. Avoid blaming or attacking, and focus on expressing your own needs and expectations.

For example, let's say your partner has a habit of interrupting you when you're trying to focus on work. You've set a boundary around your need for uninterrupted work time, but they keep barging in with questions or comments. Here's how you might address it:

"I know you don't mean to disrupt me, but when you come into my office while I'm working, it breaks my concentration and makes it harder for me to focus. I need you to respect my work time and wait until I'm available to talk unless it's an emergency. Can we agree on a signal that I'm not to be disturbed, like closing my office door?"

Notice how this response is firm but kind. It acknowledges the other person's intentions while clearly restating the boundary and requesting a specific change in behavior.

Of course, not everyone will respond positively to boundary enforcement. Some people may get defensive, dismiss your concerns, or even lash out in anger. In these cases, it's important to stay grounded in your own truth and not take their reaction personally.

Remember, you are not responsible for other people's emotions or behavior. You are only responsible for communicating your needs clearly and consistently. If someone repeatedly disrespects your boundaries despite your best efforts, it may be time to reevaluate the relationship and consider whether it's serving your highest good.

In some cases, boundary violations may be more serious and require a stronger response. If someone is engaging in abusive, threatening, or illegal behavior, it's important to seek help and support from a trusted friend, therapist, or even law enforcement. Your safety and well-being should always be the top priority.

Ultimately, reinforcing boundaries is a practice of self-love and self-respect. It's about honoring your own needs and trusting that you are worthy of being treated with dignity and care. The more you practice upholding your limits, the easier and more natural it will become.

Wrapping Up...

Setting and maintaining boundaries is a crucial skill for cultivating mental toughness and resilience. When you know your limits and communicate them clearly, you create a sense of safety and security that allows you to thrive in all areas of life.

Remember, boundaries are not about being selfish or uncaring. They're about taking responsibility for your own well-being and creating the conditions for healthy, mutually fulfilling relationships. By honoring your own needs and desires, you model self-respect and self-advocacy for others.

To recap, the three keys to effective boundary setting are:

- Understanding your boundaries: taking the time to reflect on your values, needs, and limits
- Setting your boundaries: communicating your limits clearly, directly, and consistently

- Reinforcing your boundaries: addressing violations promptly and firmly and seeking support when needed

With practice and patience, setting and maintaining boundaries will become second nature. You'll find yourself feeling more grounded, empowered, and resilient in the face of life's challenges.

But boundaries are just one piece of the mental toughness puzzle. In the next chapter, we'll explore another crucial component: cultivating a positive, optimistic mindset. Get ready to harness the power of your thoughts and beliefs to create the life you truly desire.

Case Study: Emily

Emily was a kind-hearted and hardworking nurse who always went above and beyond for her patients and colleagues. She regularly stayed late to cover shifts, took on extra tasks without complaint, and was the go-to person for emotional support in her unit. While her dedication was admirable, it was also taking a serious toll on her well-being.

Emily was constantly exhausted, both physically and emotionally. She had little time for her own self-care practices or hobbies, and her relationships outside of work were suffering. She frequently felt resentful and unappreciated, but she didn't know how to say no or advocate for her own needs.

One day, after a particularly grueling shift, Emily broke down in tears in the break room. Her supervisor, who had noticed Emily's increasing stress levels, sat down with her and gently asked what was going on. Through sobs, Emily shared how overwhelmed and depleted she felt, as if she were pouring from an empty cup.

Emily's supervisor listened with compassion and then asked a powerful question: "What boundaries do you need to set to take better care of yourself?" This question stopped Emily in her tracks. She had never really thought about her own boundaries before, always putting others' needs before her own.

With her supervisor's encouragement, Emily started to reflect on what she needed to feel more balanced and resilient. She realized that she needed to limit her overtime hours, take regular breaks during her shifts, and be more selective about which extra tasks she took on. She also recognized that she needed to carve out more time for her personal life and self-care.

Armed with this new self-awareness, Emily began to communicate her boundaries more clearly and consistently. When a colleague asked her to cover an extra shift at the last minute, she kindly but firmly explained that she had already made plans for her day off and couldn't accommodate the request. When a patient's family member started to vent excessively about personal issues, Emily gently redirected the conversation and suggested some counseling resources.

At first, setting these boundaries felt awkward and uncomfortable for Emily. She worried that others would see her as selfish or uncaring. However, as she practiced expressing her limits with respect and compassion, she found that most people were understanding and supportive. In fact, many of her colleagues expressed admiration for her self-advocacy and started to follow her lead in setting their own boundaries.

Over time, Emily began to notice significant improvements in her well-being and resilience. With more time for rest, self-care, and personal pursuits, she had more energy and focus at work. She was able to be more fully present with her patients and colleagues without the underlying resentment or depletion she had previously felt.

Emily's boundaries also had a positive ripple effect on her relationships outside of work. She was able to be a more attentive and supportive partner, friend, and family member because she wasn't constantly drained by overextending herself. She even inspired some of her loved ones to examine and communicate their own boundaries more effectively.

Of course, setting and maintaining boundaries wasn't always easy for Emily. There were times when people pushed back against her limits or tried to make her feel guilty for prioritizing her own needs. In these moments, Emily had to dig deep and remind herself that her boundaries were not only valid but necessary for her long-term health and happiness.

Through her journey, Emily learned that boundaries are not about building walls or shutting others out. They're about creating the conditions for more authentic, sustainable, and mutually nourishing relationships. By honoring her own limits and needs, she was able to show up more fully and compassionately for the people and causes she cared about most.

Emily's story is a powerful reminder that setting boundaries is not selfish but an act of self-love and respect. When we have the courage to communicate our needs and limits clearly, we create space for greater joy, connection, and resilience in all areas of our lives. With practice and patience, we can all learn to set and maintain the boundaries we need to thrive.

EIGHT

Step #7: Positivity Powers– Cultivating Optimism

 It is not the mountain we conquer but ourselves.

Edmund Hillary

I n this final step of our 7-step journey to mental toughness, we turn to one of the most powerful tools in your arsenal: optimism. Optimism isn't just about putting on a happy face —it's a fundamental way of perceiving and interacting with the world that has profound effects on your mental strength and well-being. In this chapter, you'll learn what it really means to be optimistic, the incredible benefits it bestows, and concrete strategies to cultivate an optimistic outlook, even in the face of adversity. By the end, you'll feel empowered to harness the power of positivity to enhance your mental toughness like never before.

The Power of Optimism

What exactly is optimism? At its core, optimism is the belief that things will generally work out for the best. It's a positive mindset that interprets experiences, events, and the future in a hopeful, confident light. Optimists tend to view challenges as temporary setbacks rather than permanent disasters. They believe in their ability to overcome obstacles and expect good things to happen.

This positive outlook isn't just feel-good fluff—optimism has measurable benefits for both mental and physical health. Research (Conversano et al., 2010) has linked optimism to

- lower rates of depression and anxiety
- better coping skills during hardships and times of stress
- improved cardiovascular health and immune function
- longer life span and greater overall well-being

Optimism acts as a buffer against life's inevitable difficulties. When you expect positive outcomes, you're more likely to take productive actions and persist in the face of challenges. In contrast, pessimists tend to give up more easily and slip into passivity or despair.

In terms of mental toughness specifically, optimism is like rocket fuel. It enables you to

- persevere through setbacks, disappointments, and failures
- bounce back from adversity with renewed determination
- maintain confidence and motivation when the going gets tough
- find creative solutions and opportunities amid obstacles

With an optimistic mindset, you stay focused on possibilities rather than dwelling on problems. You view hardships as temporary and specific rather than permanent and pervasive. This allows you to maintain perspective and keep moving forward even when things are difficult.

Furthermore, optimism improves your life across the board. Research shows that compared to pessimists, optimists tend to

- earn higher incomes and experience greater career success
- have more satisfying, trusting, and long-lasting relationships
- be viewed as more likable, charismatic, and influential by others
- enjoy better physical health and recover faster from illness/injury
- experience greater happiness, well-being, and overall life satisfaction

Because optimists expect positive outcomes, they're more likely to take calculated risks and keep striving toward their goals rather than giving up prematurely. They also tend to invest in their relationships, take care of their health, and make choices that create self-fulfilling prophecies of success and well-being.

Overall, tapping into the power of optimism is one of the most effective ways to upgrade your mental strength and quality of life. Optimism creates an upward spiral of positive thoughts, feelings, behaviors, and outcomes. It's not about ignoring reality or denying negative aspects of a situation. Rather, it's about intentionally shifting your focus toward what is good, what is possible, and what you can control. Here's how to cultivate this transformative mindset:

Solution #1: Honing a Positive Mindset

If you tend to be more of a "glass half empty" kind of thinker, don't despair—you absolutely can train your brain to be more positive.

It just takes consistent effort and practice to overcome entrenched negative thinking patterns.

The first step is to become aware of your explanatory style—the habitual ways in which you interpret and make sense of events. Pessimists have a negative explanatory style, characterized by the 3 P's:

- **Permanence:** Viewing negative situations as permanent and unchangeable. E.g., "I'll never find love because I'm unlovable."
- **Pervasiveness:** Globalizing negative events and allowing them to pervade all areas of life. E.g., "I failed that test, which means I'm a failure in general."
- **Personalization:** Blaming oneself and taking things personally. E.g., "It's all my fault that the project failed."

To shift toward a more positive mindset, practice catching and reframing these types of thoughts:

- Challenge permanence by reminding yourself that most situations are temporary. Look for examples of how you've overcome similar challenges before or how others have navigated this type of situation successfully. Ask yourself, "How might this change or resolve over time?"
- Combat pervasiveness by keeping things in perspective. Recognize that one negative event doesn't have to dictate your entire life experience. Compartmentalize by identifying areas of your life that are going well despite this adversity. Ask yourself, "What parts of my life are still good right now?"
- Reduce personalization by considering external factors and cutting yourself some slack. Acknowledge your role in

the situation without engaging in self-blame. Practice self-compassion and talk to yourself like a good friend would. Ask yourself, "How did others or circumstances contribute to this situation?"

Another effective way to cultivate a positive mindset is to intentionally focus on the good. The human brain is wired to pay more attention to negative stimuli (it's an evolutionary survival mechanism), but you can consciously override this tendency by

- regularly expressing gratitude, either privately or to others. Make a habit of noticing and appreciating the small joys, comforts, and privileges in your daily life.
- celebrating your own and others' successes, milestones, and efforts. Take time to acknowledge progress and give yourself credit for showing up.
- looking for the humor, beauty, inspiration, and humanity around you. Be on the lookout for small moments of delight throughout your day.
- surrounding yourself with positive people, messaging, and environments as much as possible. Curate your social media feed, reading material, and friend circles to be more uplifting than draining.

With repetition, you can shift your default thought patterns from negative to positive. It's like building a muscle—the more you practice optimistic thinking, the stronger and more automatic it becomes. Over time, your mind will start to scan for and expect the good, creating a self-reinforcing cycle of positivity.

Solution #2: Developing Optimism

In addition to generally honing a more positive mindset, you can proactively develop your optimism skills. The key lies in how you explain events to yourself and others.

Optimists view negative events as temporary, limited in scope, and influenced by external factors rather than solely caused by personal failings. You can develop a more optimistic mindset by challenging pessimistic thoughts, considering multiple contributing factors, and recognizing the impermanence of most situations.

Now, let's shift our focus to actionable techniques for cultivating optimism and seeing the bright side in the rest of this solution section.

With practice, your explanatory style will shift, and your capacity for optimism will grow. You'll be able to metabolize adversity more quickly and reframe challenges in a more hopeful, empowering light.

Another key optimism skill is finding the bright side or silver lining in difficult situations. Even in truly tragic circumstances, optimists look for

- glimmers of goodness, beauty, or meaning
- opportunities for growth, learning, or positive change
- things to be grateful for amid the pain and difficulty

This isn't about minimizing or denying the negative—it's about maintaining a balanced perspective. It's about recognizing that even in the darkest of times, there are still sources of light and reasons for hope.

Regularly ask yourself questions like:

- "What valuable lessons or insights might I gain from this experience?"
- "How might I use this situation as an opportunity to build a new skill or manifest a positive change?"
- "What am I discovering about my own strength, resilience, and capabilities?"
- "What am I grateful for, even in the midst of this challenge?"

Make a habit of noticing and naming the positive aspects of tough situations, no matter how small. The more you flex this optimism muscle, the more easily your mind will find the good—even on the darkest of days.

Solution #3: Optimism vs. Toxic Positivity

As you cultivate an optimistic mindset, it's important to avoid veering into the territory of toxic positivity. Genuine optimism means maintaining a realistically positive outlook while still acknowledging the full spectrum of human emotions and experiences. Toxic positivity, in contrast, is an overly simplified, one-dimensional approach that denies, minimizes, or invalidates anything perceived as negative.

Toxic positivity shows up as

- feeling guilty or ashamed for experiencing painful emotions
- suppressing or denying anger, sadness, grief, fear, etc.
- insisting on being happy and upbeat all the time
- shaming others for expressing negativity or vulnerability

- offering unhelpful platitudes like "Just stay positive!"
- avoiding difficult conversations or situations

While well-intentioned, toxic positivity can do more harm than good. It stigmatizes normal, healthy human emotions and pressures people to be inauthentic. It also prevents genuine processing of challenging experiences, which is essential for healing and growth.

Genuine optimism, on the other hand

- makes room for the full range of human emotions
- validates that it's normal and okay to feel pain/negativity sometimes
- encourages processing challenging feelings with self-compassion
- offers hope and encouragement without denying current realities
- remains forward-looking while still acknowledging the present
- focuses on what's within your control and influence

To cultivate authentic optimism without sliding into toxic positivity:

- Acknowledge the reality of your current situation and how you feel about it. Resist the urge to sugar-coat or gloss over real challenges.
- Validate your own and others' difficult emotions with understanding and compassion. Let yourself feel your feelings without judgment.
- Express challenging emotions in healthy ways, like

journaling, having honest conversations with trusted confidantes, creating art or music, etc.

- Gently redirect your mind toward positive possibilities and solutions once you've processed the initial wave of emotion. Ask yourself what beneficial actions you can take or changes you can make.
- Offer realistic hope and encouragement to yourself and others. Share messages that are empowering without being dismissive or overly simplistic.

It's a delicate dance, but with practice, you can master the balance of acknowledging difficulty while maintaining an optimistic outlook. You'll learn how to metabolize adversity with self-compassion and grace, using challenges as fuel for growth and transformation.

Optimism In Action

The inspiring story of POW Admiral James Stockdale perfectly illustrates the power of realistic optimism. Admiral Stockdale was held captive and tortured for eight years during the Vietnam War. Despite unimaginable suffering, he managed to survive the ordeal with his spirit intact and even thrive in the later years of his life.

When asked about his coping strategy in prison, Stockdale explained that he balanced realism with hope. He said "I never lost faith in the end of the story. I never doubted not only that I would get out but also that I would prevail in the end and turn the experience into the defining event of my life, which, in retrospect, I would not trade."

At the same time, Stockdale didn't indulge in blind optimism or wishful thinking. When asked, "Who didn't make it out?" he replied, "Oh, that's easy. The optimists. They were the ones who said, 'We're going to be out by Christmas.' And Christmas would come, and Christmas would go. Then they'd say, 'We're going to be out by Easter.' And Easter would come, and Easter would go. And then Thanksgiving, and then it would be Christmas again. And they died of a broken heart."

Stockdale's experience highlights the sweet spot of genuine optimism—having faith in the end of the story while also confronting current realities. It's about holding the tension between accepting what is and expecting the best moving forward. It's remaining realistically hopeful while taking full responsibility for your circumstances.

So, how can we apply the "Stockdale Paradox" in our own lives? Here are some key lessons:

- **Acknowledge the brutal facts of your current reality.** Don't deny or minimize challenges, setbacks, or painful emotions. Confront the truth head-on.
- **At the same time, maintain unwavering faith that you will ultimately prevail.** Hold onto hope and optimism even in the darkest times. Visualize the end of your story.
- **Focus on what's within your control.** Accept what you can't change and take responsibility for what you can influence. Channel your energy into positive action.
- **Find meaning and purpose in adversity.** Look for ways to learn, grow, and become a better version of yourself. Use challenges as opportunities for transformation.
- **Stay connected to your reasons for hope.** Regularly remind yourself of your strengths, values, and long-term vision. Surround yourself with relationships and resources that fuel your optimism.

By holding both realism and optimism simultaneously, you'll build authentic mental toughness—the ability to acknowledge difficulties while maintaining an empowered, proactive mindset. You'll learn to metabolize adversity into fuel for your growth and ultimate success.

Wrapping Up...

In this chapter, we explored the transformative power of optimism in cultivating unshakable mental strength and resilience. By understanding the true nature of optimism, its incredible benefits, and practical strategies for honing a positive mindset, you've gained a powerful tool to navigate life's challenges with grace and determination.

Throughout this chapter, we've covered a wealth of tools and techniques to increase your optimism, including:

- Understanding the true nature of optimism, its incredible benefits, and practical strategies for honing a positive mindset to cultivate a realistic yet hopeful outlook.
- Intentionally shifting your focus toward what is good, possible, and controllable while approaching challenges as opportunities for learning, transformation, and staying connected to your deepest values and purpose.
- Celebrating progress, radiating positivity and resilience, and inspiring others to create a ripple effect of positive change and empowerment.

Optimism is the cornerstone that ties all these skills together. By maintaining a realistic yet hopeful outlook, you'll be able to leverage your full mental and emotional capacity to overcome obstacles, learn from setbacks, and keep moving forward with unwavering determination.

As you integrate the practices and mindset shifts covered in this chapter, remember that optimism is not about denying reality or suppressing difficult emotions. Rather, it's about intentionally shifting your focus toward what is good, what is possible, and what you can control. It's about having faith in your ability to handle whatever comes your way and trusting in your capacity for growth and resilience.

Cultivating authentic optimism is a lifelong journey of choosing thoughts, beliefs, and actions that empower you to be your best self. It's about approaching challenges as opportunities for learning and transformation, staying connected to your deepest values and purpose, and inspiring others with your hopefulness and tenacity.

As you continue to flex your optimism muscle and build mental toughness, celebrate each milestone and moment of progress along the way. Remember that you already have everything you need to create a life of authentic joy, meaning, and fulfillment. Keep expecting the best while taking full responsibility for your circumstances. Stay realistically hopeful and fiercely committed to your personal growth and success.

Your optimism is a gift to yourself and to the world around you. As you radiate positivity and resilience in the face of life's challenges, you'll inspire others to rise to their highest potential as well.

The journey of mental toughness is one of continual evolution and expansion. With each challenge you overcome, each setback you learn from, and each victory you celebrate, you'll discover new depths of strength, wisdom, and resilience within yourself.

Case Study: Jasmine

Jasmine had always been a worrywart, even as a child. She constantly fretted about worst-case scenarios, from natural disasters to failing grades to social rejection. As an adult, her pessimism had become a self-fulfilling prophecy. She'd been passed over for promotions at work, had a string of unfulfilling relationships, and generally felt like she was just scraping by in life.

Jasmine's pessimism was a major factor in her struggles. She tended to blow small setbacks way out of proportion, turning minor annoyances into catastrophes in her mind. She obsessed over what was going wrong while ignoring her strengths and accomplishments. Over time, she'd developed a deep-seated belief that good things just didn't happen for her. Her motivation and confidence were at an all-time low.

One day, after yet another disappointment, Jasmine stumbled across a book on mental toughness. The chapter on optimism struck a chord. She recognized herself in the descriptions of pessimistic thinking and realized how much her negative outlook had been holding her back. She resolved to start training her brain for positivity.

At first, it felt forced and phony to look for the bright side. Jasmine's mind was so used to going down disastrous rabbit holes. But she was determined to rewire her thinking. She started a daily gratitude journal, listing at least three good things about each day, no matter how small. She caught herself catastrophizing and consciously replaced those thoughts with more realistic ones. For example, instead of "I'm going to bomb this presentation and get fired," she'd think, "I've prepared thoroughly, and even if it doesn't go perfectly, I'll survive and learn from it."

Jasmine also practiced reframing challenges as opportunities. When she was passed up for a promotion, instead of spiraling into despair, she thought, "This is a chance to get feedback on where I can improve so I'm in an even stronger position next time." When her car broke down, she told herself, "I can handle this. It's a hassle, but I'll figure it out, and maybe I'll discover a great new mechanic in the process."

Slowly but surely, Jasmine's default way of viewing the world started to shift. It became more natural to find the silver linings and expect positive outcomes. She felt lighter, more hopeful, and energetic. Her newfound optimism gave her the courage to take on challenges she would have shied away from before. She applied for a stretch role at work and got it. She said yes to new social opportunities and expanded her circle of friends.

As Jasmine's life started to transform for the better, she realized how much her past pessimism had been clouding her perceptions. Had the world changed? Or had her view of it changed? Sure, bad things still happen sometimes, but she no longer let them define her. She could acknowledge negativity without getting lost in it. Her newfound optimism was like a buoy, allowing her to ride the waves of life's ups and downs with so much more ease and confidence.

There were moments when Jasmine caught herself sliding back into old negative thought patterns. When this happened, she knew she had to be deliberate about shifting her mindset. She'd take some deep breaths, recall her gratitude list, and gently steer her thoughts in a more optimistic direction. Sometimes, she'd reach out to an encouraging friend or do something kind for someone else, both guaranteed mood boosters.

Over time, Jasmine realized that optimism wasn't about denying life's difficulties; it was about choosing a life-giving perspective in the midst of them. Her positive outlook became a source of incredible resilience, allowing her to rebound from setbacks and keep striving toward her goals with confidence and hope.

No, her life wasn't perfect. Yes, she still felt pessimistic sometimes. But Jasmine had learned how to catch and reframe those thoughts before they could spiral out of control. She'd discovered that her mindset was a powerful tool she could use to shape her experience of the world. And as she focused more and more on the good, the good just kept growing.

NINE

Bonus Chapter—Assertiveness Training 101

 Out of difficulties grow miracles.

Jean de la Bruyere

Throughout our journey of mastering mental toughness, we've explored a wide array of strategies and techniques to help you cultivate unshakable resilience and inner strength. From overcoming overthinking to honing emotional agility to practicing optimism, you now have a robust toolkit to navigate life's challenges with grace and determination.

In this bonus chapter, we'll dive into one final skill that can take your mental toughness to the next level: assertiveness. Assertiveness is the ability to express your thoughts, feelings, and needs in a clear, direct, and respectful manner. It's about standing up for yourself, setting healthy boundaries, and communicating with confidence and integrity.

When you're assertive, you're able to advocate for your wants and needs without resorting to aggression or passivity. You can handle difficult conversations and conflicts with poise and effectiveness, staying true to yourself while also respecting others. Assertiveness is a key component of mental toughness because it allows you to navigate interpersonal challenges with courage, resilience, and self-assuredness.

In this chapter, you'll learn the core principles and techniques of assertiveness training, a powerful approach to building assertiveness skills. We'll explore the benefits of being assertive, common barriers to assertiveness, and practical strategies you can start using today to communicate with greater clarity, confidence, and impact. By the end of this chapter, you'll have everything you need to assert yourself effectively in any situation, from the boardroom to the living room.

What Is Assertiveness Training?

At its core, assertiveness training is a type of behavior therapy designed to help individuals develop the skills to express their thoughts, feelings, and needs in a direct, honest, and appropriate way. It's about learning to communicate with confidence and respect, setting healthy boundaries, and standing up for oneself without resorting to aggression, manipulation, or passivity.

Assertiveness training typically involves a combination of cognitive, emotional, and behavioral techniques, such as:

- identifying and challenging limiting beliefs and assumptions
- practicing self-awareness and emotional regulation
- developing effective communication skills, both verbal and nonverbal
- roleplaying difficult conversations and scenarios
- setting and maintaining healthy boundaries

- cultivating a growth mindset and self-acceptance

Through assertiveness training, individuals learn to replace passive, aggressive, or passive-aggressive communication styles with assertive ones. They develop the confidence to express themselves authentically and the resilience to handle conflicts and negotiations with grace and effectiveness.

Benefits of Assertiveness Training

Developing assertiveness skills through training can have a profound impact on various aspects of life. Some of the key benefits include:

- **Improved communication and relationships:** Assertiveness enables you to express your needs and boundaries clearly, reducing misunderstandings and conflicts in personal and professional relationships.
- **Greater self-confidence and self-esteem:** By learning to stand up for yourself and communicate your worth, you develop a stronger sense of self-assurance and self-respect.
- **Enhanced decision-making and problem-solving abilities:** Assertiveness training teaches you to think critically, express your opinions confidently, and find win-win solutions in challenging situations.
- **Reduced stress and anxiety:** When you're able to advocate for your needs and manage conflicts effectively, you experience less stress and worry in interpersonal interactions.
- **Increased resilience and adaptability:** Assertiveness skills enable you to handle difficult people and situations with greater ease, bounce back from setbacks, and adapt to change more effectively.

- **Greater authenticity and integrity:** By communicating honestly and directly, you stay true to your values and build trust and respect with others.
- **Enhanced leadership and influence:** Assertive individuals are seen as more credible, charismatic, and persuasive, making them more effective leaders and change agents.

Overall, assertiveness training can help you communicate with greater clarity, confidence, and impact, improving your relationships, well-being, and success in all areas of life.

How Assertiveness Training Improves Mental Toughness

In addition to its many personal and interpersonal benefits, assertiveness training is also a powerful tool for building mental toughness. When you're assertive, you're better able to do the following:

- **Handle difficult conversations and conflicts:** With assertiveness skills, you can navigate tense interactions with composure, staying focused on solutions rather than getting derailed by emotions.
- **Advocate for yourself and your ideas:** Assertiveness empowers you to speak up for what you believe in, even in the face of opposition or skepticism, fostering greater resilience and persistence.
- **Manage stress and adversity effectively:** By communicating your needs and managing conflicts proactively, you're better equipped to handle life's challenges and bounce back from setbacks.
- **Develop greater self-awareness and emotional intelligence:** Assertiveness training requires you to tune

into your own thoughts, feelings, and values, as well as those of others, fostering greater empathy and adaptability.

- **Cultivate a growth mindset and self-acceptance:** Through assertiveness training, you learn to embrace your strengths and weaknesses, take risks, learn from failures, and communicate with authenticity and self-compassion.

In essence, assertiveness is a key pillar of mental toughness because it allows you to navigate interpersonal challenges with courage, resilience, and grace. By learning to express yourself clearly, set healthy boundaries, and advocate for your needs, you develop the inner strength and flexibility to thrive in the face of any obstacle.

Solution #1: Communication

At the heart of assertiveness training is effective communication. To express yourself assertively, you need to be able to articulate your thoughts, feelings, and needs in a clear, direct, and respectful manner. This requires a combination of self-awareness, emotional intelligence, and practical communication skills.

Assessing Your Style

The first step in improving your assertiveness is to assess your current communication style. Are you more passive, aggressive, passive-aggressive, or assertive? Consider how you typically express yourself in different situations, such as:

- giving and receiving feedback
- expressing disagreement or dissatisfaction
- making requests or saying no

- negotiating or resolving conflicts
- standing up for your ideas or beliefs

You can take self-assessments or ask for feedback from trusted friends or colleagues to get a better sense of your communication strengths and areas for improvement. Some common communication styles include:

- **Passive:** avoids expressing thoughts and feelings; goes along with others' demands; fears conflict and rejection
- **Aggressive:** expresses thoughts and feelings in a hostile, threatening way; disregards others' needs and rights
- **Passive-aggressive:** expresses thoughts and feelings indirectly through sarcasm, sabotage, or non-compliance; fears direct confrontation
- **Assertive:** expresses thoughts and feelings in an honest, direct, and respectful way; considers own and others' needs; communicates with confidence and clarity

By understanding your default communication style, you can start to identify patterns and triggers that may be holding you back from being more assertive.

Communicating Assertively

To communicate assertively, practice expressing yourself in an honest, direct, and respectful manner. Use "I" statements to take ownership of your thoughts and feelings rather than blaming or accusing others. For example:

- Instead of "You always interrupt me and don't let me finish," say, "I feel disrespected when I'm interrupted. I need to be able to express my thoughts fully."

- Instead of "Your idea won't work," say, "I have concerns about the feasibility of that approach. Can we explore some alternative solutions?"
- Focus on being specific, objective, and solution-oriented in your communication. Avoid generalizations, exaggerations, or personal attacks. Use a calm, confident tone of voice and maintain open, engaged body language.

When communicating assertively, it's also important to listen actively and empathetically to others. Show that you hear and understand their perspective, even if you disagree. Look for win-win solutions that consider everyone's needs and concerns.

Some key phrases for assertive communication include:

- "I think/feel/need..."
- "What are your thoughts on..."
- "My understanding is... Is that accurate?"
- "How can we resolve this in a way that works for both of us?"
- "I appreciate your perspective. Here's another way of looking at it..."
- Saying "No"

One of the most important assertiveness skills is the ability to say no respectfully. As we talked about back in Chapter 7, setting and maintaining healthy boundaries is essential for protecting your time, energy, and well-being. When someone makes a request or demand that doesn't align with your needs or values, practice expressing your limits clearly and firmly.

For example:

- "I appreciate you thinking of me for this project, but I don't have the bandwidth to take on any extra commitments right now."
- "I understand you're in a tight spot, but I'm not comfortable lending money. Let's brainstorm some other resources that could help."
- "I know you're eager to spend more time together, but I need some alone time this weekend to recharge. How about we plan something for next week?"

Remember that saying no doesn't make you selfish or uncaring. It's a sign of self-respect and personal integrity. By setting boundaries assertively, you create the space to focus on what truly matters to you and show up as your best self in your relationships and responsibilities.

Solution #2: Body Language

In addition to verbal communication, nonverbal cues also play a significant role in assertiveness. Your body language, facial expressions, and tone of voice can reinforce or undermine your message, affecting how others perceive and respond to you. By aligning your nonverbal communication with your assertive intentions, you can convey confidence, credibility, and respect in any interaction.

How Body Language Improves Communication

Research shows that nonverbal cues account for a significant portion of our communication impact. Some studies suggest that body language and tone of voice convey over 90% of our message, while the actual words account for less than 10% (Park & Park, 2018).

When your nonverbal communication aligns with your verbal message, it enhances your overall effectiveness and persuasiveness. Confident, open body language signals that you believe in what you're saying and can be trusted. On the other hand, closed or submissive body language can undermine your credibility and authority, even if your words are assertive.

Some key body language cues that can improve your assertive communication include:

- maintaining good eye contact (without staring or glaring)
- standing or sitting up straight with your shoulders back
- keeping your arms uncrossed and your hands visible
- using open, expansive gestures to emphasize key points
- smiling genuinely to convey warmth and friendliness
- nodding to show understanding and engagement
- mirroring the other person's body language to build rapport

Open vs. Closed Body Language

In assertiveness training, it's important to understand the difference between open and closed body language. Open body language conveys confidence, receptivity, and engagement, while closed body language signals defensiveness, resistance, or disinterest.

Examples of open body language include:

- facing the person you're speaking with directly
- maintaining an open, upright posture

- keeping your arms and legs uncrossed
- making appropriate eye contact
- using fluid, expansive gestures

In contrast, closed body language may involve:

- crossing your arms or legs tightly
- hunching or slouching
- avoiding eye contact or looking down
- fidgeting or tapping nervously
- turning your body away from the other person

To communicate assertively, aim to adopt an open, engaged posture that signals your confidence and receptivity. Avoid defensive or submissive stances that may undermine your message.

Body Language for Assertiveness

In addition to general open and engaging body language, there are specific nonverbal cues that can enhance your assertiveness in communication:

- Stand or sit up straight, with your shoulders back and your head held high. This posture conveys confidence and self-assurance.
- Make direct eye contact, holding the other person's gaze for a few seconds at a time. This signals your engagement and sincerity.
- Use expansive, purposeful gestures to emphasize key points. For example, you might use your hands to indicate size or importance, or point to visual aids.
- Speak in a clear, steady voice, enunciating your words and

varying your tone and inflection to add impact. Avoid mumbling, trailing off, or speaking too quickly.

- Maintain a neutral or pleasant facial expression, smiling warmly when appropriate. Avoid scowling, frowning, or rolling your eyes, which can come across as aggressive or dismissive.
- Take up space by standing or sitting with your feet shoulder-width apart and your arms relaxed at your sides. Avoid making yourself small or constricted.

Remember, the goal is to convey confidence, openness, and respect through your body language. By aligning your nonverbal cues with your assertive message, you reinforce your credibility and effectiveness in any interaction.

Solution #3: Emotional Management

Effective assertiveness requires not only clear communication and confident body language but also emotional intelligence and self-regulation. When you're able to manage your emotions effectively, you can stay grounded, focused, and respectful even in challenging or high-stakes situations. Emotional management is a key skill for assertiveness and overall mental toughness.

How Emotional Management Improves Assertiveness

Emotions play a powerful role in communication and relationships. When you're in touch with your own feelings and able to regulate them effectively, you're better able to

- express yourself clearly and authentically
- listen actively and empathetically to others
- stay calm and focused in the face of stress or conflict

- advocate for your needs and boundaries respectfully
- build and maintain trust and rapport with others

On the other hand, when emotions are running high and unchecked, they can derail even the most well-intentioned assertiveness efforts. Anger, fear, or defensiveness can lead to aggressive or passive-aggressive communication, while anxiety or self-doubt can result in passivity or avoidance.

By developing emotional intelligence and self-regulation skills, you can communicate assertively, even in emotionally charged situations. You're able to

- recognize and label your own emotions accurately
- understand the triggers and root causes of your feelings
- express your emotions in healthy, constructive ways
- manage stress and maintain composure under pressure
- empathize with and respond to others' emotions skillfully

Ultimately, emotional management allows you to approach challenging conversations and conflicts with greater clarity, confidence, and resilience. You're able to assert yourself effectively while also maintaining positive relationships and outcomes.

How to Regulate Emotions in Conversation

To communicate assertively in high-stakes or emotionally charged situations, try these strategies for regulating your emotions:

- **Take a pause and breathe deeply.** Before responding, take a few slow, deep breaths to calm your physiological arousal and clear your mind.

- **Label your emotions accurately.** Take a moment to identify what you're feeling without judgment. Naming your emotions helps to diffuse their intensity and gives you greater clarity and control.
- **Identify your triggers and hot buttons.** Notice what specific words, actions, or situations tend to provoke a strong emotional reaction in you. Anticipating these triggers can help you regulate your response more effectively.
- **Express your feelings constructively.** Use "I" statements to express your emotions in a clear, non-blaming way. For example, "I feel frustrated when..." or "I'm concerned about..."
- **Empathize with the other person's perspective.** Try to put yourself in the other person's shoes and understand their feelings and needs. Expressing empathy can help diffuse defensiveness and build rapport.
- **Focus on solutions and common ground.** Instead of getting stuck in emotional reactions, direct the conversation toward finding mutually beneficial solutions. Look for areas of agreement and shared goals.
- **Know when to take a break.** If emotions are running too high to have a productive conversation, suggest taking a break and returning to the discussion later. Use this time to process your feelings and regain your composure.

By practicing these emotional regulation strategies, you can assert yourself more effectively, even in challenging or contentious situations. You'll be able to express your needs and perspectives clearly while also maintaining your cool and building positive relationships.

Wrapping Up...

In this bonus chapter, we explored the power of assertiveness training for building mental toughness and resilience. By developing the skills to express yourself clearly, confidently, and respectfully, you can navigate any interpersonal challenge with greater ease and effectiveness.

We covered the key components of assertiveness training, including:

- assessing and improving your communication style
- practicing assertive verbal communication techniques
- aligning your body language with your assertive message
- managing your emotions effectively in high-stakes situations

Assertiveness is a crucial skill for mental toughness because it allows you to advocate for your needs, set healthy boundaries, and communicate with impact and integrity. When you're able to express yourself assertively, you build greater self-awareness, confidence, and resilience in all areas of life.

As we close out this comprehensive guide to mastering mental toughness, remember that building inner strength and resilience is an ongoing journey. Continue to practice and integrate the strategies and techniques covered in each chapter, from silencing your inner critic to cultivating optimism to communicating assertively. Stay committed to your personal growth and celebrate your progress along the way.

Share the Power of the 7-Step Transformation

As you turn the last pages of this book, I hope you are already feeling the powerful changes that arise when you take a proactive approach to your health and well-being. Habits take around 66 days to form, so make it a point to practice the strategies contained in this book until they form part of your daily life.

If this book has helped you feel more positive, set healthy boundaries, and prioritize your time, I hope you can share just one or two sentences about its impact on your life.

Thanks once again. May you continue to feel empowered, inspired, and equipped to see every challenge as a vital opportunity for growth.

Scan the QR code

Conclusion

As we come to the end of our journey through the world of mental toughness, I hope you're feeling empowered, inspired, and equipped with the tools and strategies you need to build unshakable resilience and inner strength.

Throughout this book, we've explored the key components of mental toughness, from mastering your mindset to embracing challenges to communicating assertively. We've delved into the science behind peak performance and the psychology of resilience, and we've practiced proven techniques for overcoming adversity and achieving your goals.

You've learned how to silence your inner critic, cultivate optimism, and reframe setbacks as opportunities for growth. You've discovered the power of self-awareness, emotional agility, and healthy habits for managing stress and maintaining focus. Most importantly, you've gained the confidence and self-assurance to take bold action, speak your truth, and stay true to your values, no matter what obstacles come your way.

But remember, mastering mental toughness is not a one-time event but a lifelong journey of growth and self-discovery. It's about consistently choosing to show up as your best self, even in the face of fear, doubt, or adversity. It's about embracing the discomfort of change and the uncertainty of new challenges, knowing that this is where true strength and resilience are forged.

As you continue on your path to greater mental toughness, be patient and compassionate with yourself. Celebrate your progress, learn from your setbacks, and surround yourself with supportive people who inspire and challenge you to keep growing. Stay curious, stay committed, and stay true to your unique journey.

Remember, you are stronger than you know. You have the power to overcome any obstacle, achieve any goal, and create the life you desire. You have everything you need to thrive and succeed, not just in spite of challenges but because of them.

So keep honing your mental muscles, keep reaching for your highest potential, and keep shining your light in the world. Your mental toughness is not just a gift to yourself but to everyone around you, inspiring others with your courage, resilience, and unwavering spirit.

Thank you for joining me on this transformative journey of self-discovery and empowerment. It has been an honor to share these insights and strategies with you, and I hope they serve you well as you continue to master your mindset and unleash your inner strength.

Here's to your unbreakable mental toughness, your limitless potential, and your most fulfilling, purposeful life. Keep rising, keep shining, and keep embracing the power of your indomitable will. The world needs your unique brand of strength, resilience, and courage more than ever.

References

Allende, I. (2024). *Isabel Allende quotes.* Southern Living. https://www.southernliving.com/culture/quotes-about-strength

Charney, D. S. (2003). The psychobiology of resilience and vulnerability to anxiety disorders: implications for prevention and treatment. *Dialogues in Clinical Neuroscience,* *5*(3), 207–221. https://www.ncbi.nlm.nih.gov/pmc/articles/PMC3181630/

Conversano, C., Rotondo, A., Lensi, E., Della Vista, O., Arpone, F., & Reda, M. A. (2010). Optimism and its impact on mental and physical well-being. *Clinical Practice & Epidemiology in Mental Health,* *6*(1), 25–29. https://doi.org/10.2174/1745017901006010025

Bruyere J. (2024). *Jean de la Bruyere quotes.* Southern Living. https://www.southernliving.com/culture/quotes-about-strength

Dweck, C. (2012). *Mindset: How you can fulfill your potential.* Robinson.

Gibran. K. (2024). *Khalil Gibran quotes.* Southern Living. https://www.southernliving.com/culture/quotes-about-strength

Hello Driven. *The 50 Best Resilience Quotes.* February 20, 2019. https://home.hellodriven.com/articles/the-50-best-resilience-quotes/

Hillary. E. (2024). *Edmund Hillary quotes.* Southern Living. https://www.southernliving.com/culture/quotes-about-strength

King, M.L. Jr. (2024). *Martin Luther King Jr. quotes.* Southern Living. https://www.southernliving.com/culture/quotes-about-strength

Lange, K. (2020, February 3). *Medal of honor Monday: Navy Vice Adm. James Stockdale.* U.S. Department of Defense. https://www.defense.gov/News/Feature-Stories/story/Article/2097870/medal-of-honor-monday-navy-vice-adm-james-stockdale/

Mandela, N. (2024). *Nelson Mandela quotes.* Southern Living. https://www.southernliving.com/culture/quotes-about-strength

Marley. B. (2024). *Bob Marley quotes.* Southern Living. https://www.southernliving.com/culture/quotes-about-strength

Park, S. G., & Park, K. H. (2018). Correlation between nonverbal communication and objective structured clinical examination score in medical students. *Korean Journal of Medical Education,* *30*(3), 199–208. https://doi.org/10.3946/kjme.2018.94

Porter, C., Palmier-Claus, J., Branitsky, A., Mansell, W., Warwick, H., & Varese, F.

(2019). Childhood adversity and borderline personality disorder: a meta-analysis. *Acta Psychiatrica Scandinavica*, *141*(1), 6–20. https://doi.org/10.1111/acps.13118

Uchtdorf, D. F. (2024). *Dieter F. Uchtdorf quotes*. Southern Living. https://www.southernliving.com/culture/quotes-about-strength